Dr. Sean M. Carton, Andres Zapata
and Peter Meacham
Edited by Matt McDermott

UNIVERSITY X:

How to rescue a college
brand from bland.

ISBN 978-0-9890136-0-4

Proudly published in
Baltimore, MD, USA.
www.idfive.com

TABLE OF CONTENTS

Introduction

REMEMBER the old TV commercials for laundry detergents? The ones where the name brand would go up against the nefarious Brand X. The faceless, nameless, thoroughly unappealing Brand X. It served as the foil for the hero product. Everything it could do, our name brand detergent could do brighter, whiter, better.

Brand X was the patron saint of average. The iconic patsy for the unimpressive. A boring, underwhelming control against which every name brand came out on top.

Really, Brand X's biggest sin wasn't its lack of quality. It was its inherent lack of impact. In a crowded market, that's a death sentence.

Unfortunately, higher ed is filled with its fair share of Brand X's, schools that have failed to craft a message that sets them apart from their competition. Schools that haven't figured out how to reach students and spark action. Schools anchored by inertia—whether unknowingly or through internal politics—unable to keep up with the quickly changing trends and attitudes in higher ed.

They're University X's. The educational marketplace is filled with them. And with the growing popularity of online and for-profit education, it's getting even fuller.

In today's increasingly competitive world of higher education, any institutional communications or admissions professional who isn't fighting every day—heck, every minute—against the prospect of their institution becoming the next University X is surrendering to a bleak future indeed.

Wondering if your school may already be venturing into University X territory? Try the Thumb Test. Place your thumb over the logo on an ad, a website, a poster—anything that you use to market your school. Now ask yourself honestly, "Would our target audiences know without a doubt that this is promoting our school?" If you can't answer "Yes", then it's time to get to work. A word of warning: It won't be as straightforward as you might think.

A school's brand is more than just branding

"Branding" is one of those words that many use. But few agree on its definition. To some, branding means a mark or a visual representation of an organization, a logo or a typeface. To others, branding is that ineffable feeling you get from an organization—whether good or bad. Other folks see branding as something that has to do with building awareness for a product or company.

The reality is that none of these are entirely right. Just about everyone agrees that a brand has personality, emotion, experience; it has characteristics, values and attributes that need to be defined, honored and protected.

To survive, college brands must exist beyond the marketing department.

But we want you to view your brand beyond the conventional definition. For too long, schools have relied on the marketing department to nurture and protect the brand. But there's a problem with that. The marketing folks aren't the ones responding to a student's request for more information. They're not the ones responsible for guiding how a professor interacts with students. They're not the one's working to create new platforms for distance learning. Every encounter a student or stakeholder has with the school beyond marketing initiatives plays just as important a role in brand perception as the marketing effort itself.

To survive, college brands must exist beyond the marketing department. Beyond the admissions department. Beyond even the administration. It has to be an all-encompassing commitment to look at every student touch point, every faculty interaction, and every stakeholder conversation as a larger part of the total brand. And while many universities have wonderful brands in the traditional sense, they're shortsighted; many are unable to see their brand as more than the marketing they use to promote student enrollment. While they may not look like University X, these universities sure act like University X.

Wondering how your school can break out of the University X vortex, or avoid becoming a University X in the first place? We have a few ideas. Based on our decades of experience marketing, managing and teaching in the higher education marketplace, this book approaches the greatest challenges facing colleges today from a variety of angles, melding art and science, emotion and data. We propose that a school's brand will live or die based on the ability to find new allies inside the university—and new inspiration outside the industry.

Easy to say. Much harder to do. We have to face reality: if you can't look at your brand as being something bigger than branding, it will flop. Worse yet, no one will even pay enough attention to notice it has flopped.

So here's our effort to expand your idea of what brand really means. We've centered our extended definition of brand in these chapters:

Strategy

This chapter covers marketing approaches that support your brand in the more traditional and tactical sense. Along with design and media, you'll have the most control over this. It's essential you get it right.

If you can't look at your brand as being something bigger than branding, it will flop. Worse yet, no one will even pay enough attention to notice it has flopped.

Design

Yes, this is the visual side of your brand, but we dive deeper. We tackle the idea of design from multiple perspectives: brand perception, consumer action, credibility-building, interactive best practices, and more.

Media

This is as much about the choice of media channels you use as it is how you use them. And while it might not seem obvious, how you use and manage your media directly impacts your brand. Schools that use media in new or more efficient ways tend to have a strong brand to match. How you approach your media is as much a barometer of your brand's health as it is a contributor to its success.

Data

It's no surprise. Data is driving more and more of our decisions. How we collect it, how we use it, and how we protect it have a greater impact on how a brand is perceived, internally and externally, than even a decade ago. And with continual emphasis on online transactions and education, its role will only get bigger.

Recruitment

Brand is threaded throughout the recruitment process, particularly from the promotional side. But it's just as contingent on the responsiveness, flexibility and cooperation of the various departments tasked with handling the student relationship as it is with the marketing materials themselves. Brand perception can break down at any point in the student decision process if everyone isn't on the same page.

Big Ideas

These are our ruminations not only on the state of higher ed marketing, but on business in general. We'll explore some of the latest evolutions in how people are pursuing advanced educations—and offer some suggestions for how to prepare your school (and by extension, its brand) for a future that brings the most disruptive changes our industry has ever seen.

This book is meant to be the vaccine for University X. Within these pages you'll find strategies and tactics for smart, integrated marketing, sound recruitment strategies, and the information you'll need to guide the ongoing choreography of data and emotion. We hope these ideas, strategies, and techniques will catalyze your efforts to better identify your audience, improve awareness, drive admissions, and enhance the world's perception of your institution.

Welcome! And say goodbye to University X.

Strategy

OF course, it doesn't hurt to start with strategy. Without it, how will you ever know when you are done or if it worked? To many, "establishing a brand" sounds a little like voodoo or (perhaps even worse) something that consumer packaged goods companies have to worry about. Usually it's because the processes behind it are rarely laid out in a way that makes sense to the communications team. The processes fail to address just how they'll help the school accomplish its goals.

The best strategies are the simplest ones. Don't mistake simple with easy or dumb. We mean simple as in clear, realistic, communicable, and accessible. And since we sometimes forget that a strategy is the response to a goal, the better strategies are the ones forged from simple goals. Clear goals such as reduce attrition by 15% over the next five years, increase enrollment by 7% each year over the next three years, increase brand awareness in our region by 10%, or recruit and enroll the inaugural class of 50 students for a new program are goals that stand a chance.

Strategies are inspired by the objective they are trying to accomplish and grounded by the reality of budget, time, audience, competition, brand flexibility, and differentiation.

It's true, a lot goes into branding and strategy. It includes externally focused market research to determine the needs of constituent segments. It's also internally focused research that uncovers your school's true value and positioning. At the core, branding and strategic development depend on finding a voice that cuts through the noise and positioning the brand when and where your target audience will hear it.

The voice must be genuine. It must be able to elicit emotional responses. It has to be honest. And it has to help you get closer to your desired outcomes. The quality of the methods behind the research will determine whether you end up with valid, reliable messages or more empty noise. In the end, whatever your tactic or approach, it all comes back to strategy.

The Truth about Branding

BRANDING is not about altering reality; it's about owning it. Needless to say, that's easier said than done. You can't fake it. First and foremost, your brand needs to align with the reality of your experience and the perceptions of your audiences. No surprise, when we're talking about brand, we're not centering our discussion on logos and typefaces. We're talking the overall experience.

Today, more than ever before, brands are collaborations. They're the sum total of the "official" story you put out through your marketing and communications combined with what your students and prospects are saying about you online. The key to great brands these days isn't to spin the truth or hide from the criticism. It's to find harmony between the three main dimensions of your brand.

No surprise, when we're talking about brand, we're not centering our discussion on logos and typefaces. We're talking the overall experience.

Your Perceived Brand: The way people currently see your brand, whether correct or not;

Your Actual Brand: The actual state of your brand. In many situations, this differs from the perceived brand simply because the strategy to accurately communicate the true attributes has been muddy and inconsistent; and

Your Desired Brand: The way you'd like your brand to be perceived moving forward.

Often, these don't align. For example, audiences may see your school as a low-cost alternative to your competition—with a lower tier quality of education to match. In actuality, you may be more affordable, and your programs may be just as good if not better than the competition. But you desire for your brand to be looked at as a university that offers top tier programs at a great value. To find alignment of all three perspectives, we suggest you work to **SNAG** your audiences: Surprise, Nurture, Action, Grasp.

Surprise

It's incredibly difficult to break through firmly held preconceptions, especially when it comes to preconceptions formed by the ever-powerful medium that is "word of mouth." In order to blast through the prejudices your customers and prospects might harbor, it's important to present a bold, truthful image that challenges conventional wisdom. Show things how they really are, especially characteristics of your brand. These may be values that may fly under the radar because you take them for granted but are nonetheless an essential element of your institution's "DNA". What really jolts people into a new mindset? The surprising truths.

Some Surprising Facts

- Roughly more than 68% of Facebook users are over 35.[1]
- Social networking sites are the least likely place a consumer will go to research a product or service (company websites are the most popular choice).[2]
- Nearly 85% of US Internet users view online video every month.[3]
- Even if you have great organic search engine placement, paid search can increase your site traffic by as much as 50%.[4]

Nurture

Just encouraging people to learn more about you is asking them to make a commitment. People don't like commitments. Especially with brands. They'll be reluctant; don't come on too strong. Guide and nurture your audiences through small nudges, well timed assistance with logistics, and persuasive, useful content that allows them to see themselves as having made the decision on their own. Establish a content strategy that offers prospects information, entertainment, or advice that makes their lives better—but that also aligns with what your brand is all about.

Nurturing Your Prospects

- A lead contacted within five minutes is 22 times more likely to convert than one contacted after 30 minutes.[5]
- If you're trying to contact a lead, keep trying: there's a 93% chance you'll make contact after six tries versus only a 39% chance on the first try.[6]
- Watch out for ghosts. A 2010 survey found that one third of first year applicants and 50% of transfer applicants didn't identify themselves until submitting an application.[7]
- Consumers who visit branded online communities are there to read content (27.3%) and follow others' posts (18.8%). It's definitely worth nurturing these folks: 82.6% of them report that they'd be willing to become brand advocates.[8]

Action

We all know that people are resistant to change. Most won't take action unless the outcome is assured…and has an obvious benefit. Without a clear and present directive, people procrastinate. They choose inaction over action, even if the value is staring them in the face. To move your prospects from initial interest to action, you need to engage them first. Then present them with clear next steps to move them forward so they can achieve the outcome they really desire.

Encouraging Action

- Letting prospects know what's in it for them by adding a few "value" bullet points to a landing page can increase conversions by over 200%.[9]
- Simplifying your landing pages by displaying only one call to action can increase response rates nearly 400%.[10]
- Mobile advertising can generate click-through-rates up to 15 times higher than non-mobile campaigns…and they're 22% cheaper on average.[11]
- More than 61% of social media users report they want more information—not less—from companies they interact with online.[12]

Grasp

It's tough for any of us to overcome long-held beliefs and patterns of behavior. We get it. But if you're going to move prospective students forward, you have to make it easy for them to acquire new behaviors and grab hold of new beliefs. Keeping your messaging simple, respecting the time, demands, and attention of your audiences, and positioning your messaging so that it appeals to what they need (not just what you want them to know) are all-important ways to influence your target audiences and help them to grasp the value of your brand.

Help Your Audiences Grasp Your Value

- Timing is everything: several studies of email click rates have found that sending an email between 6 p.m. and 6 a.m. gives it the best chance of being opened.[13]
- Sometimes friends are the best way to get your value across: 58% of consumers reported discovering a branded online community via a friend's Facebook post (58%) versus traditional advertising (15%).[14]
- Mobile users really want relevance: One third of smartphone and tablet users cite personal relevance as the primary reason they interact with mobile advertising.[15]
- Don't underestimate the power of emotion. Nielsen found that television spots that generated an "emotional connection" with the viewer were judged by consumers to be the most likable ads.[16]

The bottom line: when it comes to branding, you have to understand your value to your customers and state it clearly so they understand what you have to offer. Only then are you in a position to SNAG them.

Integrated Marketing…Whatever that Means

ONCE upon a time, the definition of integrated marketing used to mean the classic communications trifecta—advertising, public relations, and direct marketing. Say goodbye to "once upon a time." These days, few people are clear on what integrated marketing really means.

So why is that? For one, the explosion of new-ish communications channels introduced by the Internet has obfuscated the issue. Does integrated marketing also mean creating websites? Creating mobile apps?

To put it in simple terms, integrated marketing has two major elements: coordination and flexibility.

Monitoring social media? To be integrated, do you have to be a master of *all* communications channels? Does "integrated" mean "digital + traditional?" Or does it simply mean that you'll use whatever medium you need to in order to reach your target audiences?

Aside from the buzzy sound of the expression, the term's confusion is amplified by the impact that the Internet and social media have had on how integrated marketing is (or should be) carried out.

To put it in simple terms, integrated marketing has two major elements: coordination and flexibility. These elements work together to maximize effectiveness while minimizing cost.

Coordination refers to consistent messaging and creative branding across a variety of media and communications. Flexibility refers to the ability to track, measure, and make adjustments to all of the media and marketing efforts that an organization has running at any given time.

The reason new media and technology have profoundly affected what it means to be an integrated marketer is that the process has become more complex, but also more technical. The growing diversity of media makes coordination more involved, but the trackable and fluid nature of digital media makes flexibility practical.

Billboards, TV spots, and other mass media promotions can be a great way to create brand awareness and build a reputation for your institution, but they are expensive and employ questionable metrics to test performance. Truly integrated marketing now means being hyper-targeted, measurable, and responsive to constant tweaking based on performance.

So what are some quick ways to make your school's marketing more integrated?

Start with a clearly defined goal

Though it may seem obvious, this step is frequently overlooked. Market research is great for developing a media strategy, but the first question should always be "What exactly do we want to accomplish?" A clearly defined and measurable goal would be something like: We want to boost qualified leads by 35%. Stating that you want to be known as the "best school in the country" is the *opposite* of a clear goal.

Define your audiences

Base your strategy around who and where your audiences are. If they are going to be searching for your institution, you're going to want to be there so *they* can find *you*. Save yourself a lot of time and money by focusing on those who are truly likely to care about you. Avoid chasing mass appeal. For example, if you are trying to increase the subscription base of *Home and Garden*, running a TV spot during Monday Night Football is silly, regardless of how many people will see it.

Make it accountable

The real value of an integrated marketing approach is that it is accountable. Don't settle for "Hey, look at this cool commercial we did!" Demand evidence that your efforts are not only reaching the right audience, but that they're having the desired effect. It's OK to be bottom line-oriented in your marketing. Don't let the "blue-sky, high-level creative" types convince you otherwise.

Keep it consistent

It's easy for a message to get muddied over multiple channels. Especially when multiple people are working with it. Help prevent that by identifying a torchbearer for your school's brand—and your message. Have them monitor all communications for quality and consistency. Whether an audience sees you in a paid search ad or on TV, they should have no doubt who you are and what you stand for.

Once you've clearly defined your goals, clearly defined your audience and are accountable for the results of your campaign, you've integrated your marketing.

(Post) Modern Marketing Myths: Busted

WHEN we speak at conferences, we find the most interesting part of the whole experience is the Q&A. We like it because we get challenged, and we get to hear from a broad range of marketers and communications people about what's bothering them. It's a rare glimpse of the "real world" that's often quite different than—and we mean this with great love and respect—what you hear from those of us writing about marketing.

Unfortunately a lot of the expert advice we've heard is conventional wisdom that's woefully short on convention and severely lacking in wisdom. These myths are usually stated with a large degree of certainty but are rarely backed up by anything more than anecdotal observations. While it's human nature to want to make sense of things based on your own experience, a lot of colleges (and their ad agencies) are wasting money or missing opportunities because they believe them.

Unfortunately a lot of the expert advice we've heard is conventional wisdom that's woefully short on convention and severely lacking in wisdom.

So let's take a stab at busting up a few of these common digital marketing myths.

Social media belongs to the young

This is by far one of the most common myths. In many ways, it's not unlike the arguments that people would make back in the '90s about sinking money into websites. "Well, all that techie stuff is all fine and dandy for the young folks," went the common refrain, "but our audiences are older, and they don't use that stuff."

Baloney. It was baloney then, and it's baloney now when it comes to social media.

Look at 2012 statistics[17] on social media usage and you'll see that social networking site usage for adults 18-29 has actually fallen while usage for adults over 30 continues to rise. The latest research[18] also shows that, for example, the share of Facebook users over 35 has increased to 68%. As for Twitter, more than 58% of users are over 35.

Print is dead

We usually hear this one from well-meaning people who are big believers in online marketing. We totally understand this sentiment, but it's just not smart marketing.

Print still has an important role in the overall marketing mix, as evidenced by studies that looked at catalog sales[19] and found that print catalogs are still big drivers of revenue; people like to browse print and buy online. We don't blame them: print catalogs have a greater emotional impact than an equivalent product listing on a website. Every type of media has its place and is best used for what it's best at, such as the emotional impact of print or the ease of online purchasing.

If you want to drive traffic, put all your money into online

This is another one often spouted by well-meaning true believers. However, as studies[20] show, offline media is often one of the biggest drivers of online behavior. And, interestingly enough, broadcast media—TV and radio in particular—often builds the kind of awareness that potential students need to check out a particular site. If nothing else, traditional media lowers the "click barrier" on the online leg of the campaign.

In online display advertising, it's all about the number of impressions

True, increasing your impressions will increase your exposure to your targets, but as John Burbank, CEO of Nielsen's online division so aptly puts it,[21] dishing up lots of impressions isn't enough: You also have to serve and engage your target audiences in order to reach them online.

A lot of the metrics we use to measure success of online campaigns may be wrong. Michael Zimbalist makes a compelling case in Ad Age[22] that we shouldn't be thinking about impressions at all, but rather looking at measurement using something similar to TV's gross rating point (GRP) model. For online, he suggested creating the WRP—web rating point. This involves serving up ads in a way so that they hold the user's full attention as the only marketing message on the page for a minimum of five seconds.

If you're thinking mobile, it's all about the iPhone

This one really gets to us. We've been fans of Apple since 1984, but it bugs the heck out of us that mobile has now become synonymous with iPhone in many marketers' minds.

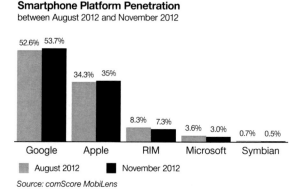

Smartphone Platform Penetration
between August 2012 and November 2012

Source: comScore MobiLens

The hype machine has convinced us that mobile apps can only be served up on iOS. But the truth is iOS holds 35% of the smartphone market (according to a January 2013 report from ComScore[23]) compared to Android's nearly 54%. If you only concentrate on the iPhone, you're missing out.

Video games are for teenage boys

The idea that only pimply-faced teenagers play video games has been with us for a long time. This misconception affects everything from video game advertising creative to how marketers think about integrating the growing video game population with advertising. According to a report by Deloitte[24], the popularity of video gaming is surging among older and more affluent populations.

Mobile advertising is [insert adjective here]

It seems like no other advertising medium is filled with as grand a set of pronouncements, as conflicting a set of data, and as much confusion as the mobile marketing biz.

There's data[25] to show that mobile advertising far surpasses online advertising in terms of effective ROI. Of course, just a few years ago some studies[26] indicated a heck of a lot of consumers didn't even know they could get online with their phones. The Interactive Advertising Bureau says that mobile is fantastic for driving brand awareness[27], and still other folks see mobile as the future of marketing[28].

Who's right? Probably everyone...and no one. Speaking of mobile as one homogenous medium is wrong. There's a dizzying array of platforms, an alphabet soup of operating systems, and huge variations in consumer sophistication when it comes to using these devices. Until the great "mobile wars" are over and we settle on a couple of operating systems and comparable experiences across devices, it's wrong to take a monolithic view of mobile marketing.

It's enough just to drive people to my site

Whoo, boy! This is another biggie when it comes to misconceptions leading to silly decisions and wasted resources.

It's not enough to drive students and prospects to your site if you're looking to capture their information, drive applications, or generate response of any kind. To be effective, you need to match your landing pages to your campaign[29].

Even then, there's a lot you can do to drive response in terms of design, copy, and the user interface. Changes (such as the "Mad Libs" form style[30] that can increase response rates 25% to 40%) can have a huge impact on response rate. Dumping people on your homepage isn't enough. There must be something driving them to act. To request more information. To apply. To share.

[Social media platform] is the place to be

This is another biggie. A particular platform or site might be big today, but history shows that putting all your eggs in one virtual basket is a bad idea. Popularity rises and wanes can be unpredictable. Audiences are always looking for the next big thing. Just ask Friendster.

There's another issue, too: Not all social media platforms are equal. They don't all share the same demographics, they're used for different things, and they're different in terms of consumer engagement. A Facebook status update isn't the same as a tweet (or vice versa), but both have their place in terms of conveying different kinds of information. Study the various platforms and use the right tool for the right job.

Everyone else is doing a better job than I am

Finally, there's the feeling that everyone else (whoever they are) is doing a better job than you when it comes to online marketing. They've got better measurement tools, more successful campaigns, and are more savvy about delivering ROI for their online media campaigns than you are.

Never fear! If you peek behind the curtain[31], you'll discover that "more than 40% of marketers don't even know whether the social media tools they're using were capable of measuring ROI!" And that's just the people who were honest enough to share the fact they didn't know something—not an easy thing to admit.

It's clear that we're all still figuring this stuff out. Anyone who tells you that they have The Answer is a fool or a snake oil salesperson.

So what's the takeaway here?

Don't be afraid to test…

Whether you're trying a new medium or refining one you've been playing with for some time, experiment with your options. Look into collecting phone numbers for mobile marketing efforts. Consider promoting the social channels of your school or its departments on traditional media.

…But don't forget to measure

Determine how you're going to gauge how successful your experiments were. Use traditional measurements like number of leads generated, but also consider alternate metrics that may provide a different degree of insight such as time people spent on your page or number of mentions generated online.

A Social Media Strategy Checklist

WHY should you spend your ad dollars on social media?

That might seem like a silly question, given that everyone seems to be shifting ad budgets to hop on the social media bandwagon. But if you aren't asking it, you're asking for disaster. And if you can't answer the question with a comprehensive, strategic answer, you're wasting your money.

A 2012 Ad Age article[32] indicates that more marketers will have their wallets open: More than a quarter of digital budgets will go to social—a significant increase from the previous year.

It's tough to read any of the industry press these days without getting the feeling that everyone's doing social media better than you are.

You'd think that would have an agency like ours giddy. But the truth is we're worried. Only rarely have we encountered people with actual strategies behind their social media push. Sure, plenty of higher ed clients (and prospects) we've spoken to over the years have made vague noises about a viral video or being on Facebook or tweeting. But when we've pressed them for why they want those things, few can give us an answer.

Not that we blame them: It's tough to read any of the industry press these days without getting the feeling that everyone's doing social media better than you are. Ad spending on social media sites keeps going up, the buzz is deafening, and just about every school you encounter asks you to follow them on Twitter, read some departmental blog, or to LIKE them on Facebook. And like any new thing, it's got that fresh sheen that's hard to resist.

But before you spend money on building or expanding your school's social media presence, take a step back. If you aren't spending money with a strategy, you're throwing it away.

Here's a 10-step social media strategy checklist to help you develop that strategy. Actually, they're questions you should be asking yourself (and your marketing team/agency). It's hardly magical stuff; you could probably apply a lot of these questions to just about any advertising or marketing you do. But going through this checklist will help you develop a strategy based on results, not hype. It may be painful, especially if you like new things, but when you're getting real results instead of making excuses, you'll be glad you did.

1. What are we trying to accomplish?

Are you looking for more leads, more direct sales, greater brand awareness, conversions, or brand engagement? Understanding what you're trying to actually do with your social media presence should be the first step in developing a social media strategy.

2. Why social media?

Is your audience there? Do you want to build stronger relationships with students and prospects? Demonstrate that you're down with the kids? Connect with a niche audience that's difficult to reach otherwise? Don't simply jump on the bandwagon. Examine why the wagon is the best way to get where you're going. Ask yourself: Is spending money on social media going to provide a better return on investment than other forms of advertising?

3. What kind of social media will help us best achieve our goals?

Do you need to utilize social networking sites, blogs, real-time updates, social news sites, media-sharing sites, review/directory sites, virtual worlds, or display ads on social media sites? In some respects, talking about a social media presence is like talking about having an advertising presence: You must specify what you're doing and where you're going to place it. Examine the characteristics of the social media venue you want your college to have a presence on.

How do those characteristics fit what you're trying to accomplish?

4. **Are we prepared to let go of control of our brand, at least a little?**

   You can't participate in social media without being, well, social. You must be willing to engage in conversations—some of them uncomfortable—with students, prospective students, alumni, donors, media, and more. But there's a funny thing about a conversation: You have to give up a degree of control to continue having one. You must come to peace with the idea that you can't monopolize or manipulate the conversation. Is your university willing to let go—and how much?

5. **What will we do to encourage participation?**

   There's nothing more embarrassing than going to a school's YouTube channel and seeing that the viral video it spent tons of money making has managed just 127 views. Ditto for going to a university Twitter feed and seeing that it has all of 11 followers. What are you planning to do to drive people to your social media presence? And do you have the money to do it? Often, traditional marketing can help with this. Advertise your Facebook account on a poster in an academic building. Send your students an email inviting them to connect on Twitter.

6. **Who will maintain our social media presence?**

   Participating in social media takes a lot of work. You must have something to say and you must have someone (or a team of people) to say it on a regular basis. In our experience, there's more than one way to succeed. For some clients, we've taken the reins, providing the content and interacting with audiences on the school's behalf, whether it's finding and posting interesting links or routing questions from prospective students to the admissions liaisons. Alternately, we've worked with schools to create a strategy that includes editorial calendars, workflows, audience analysis and monitoring. Then we've handed the keys over to internal staff, stepping in when appropriate to help tweak strategy and execution. Whichever approach you take, there must be someone to own it. Do you have staff ready to commit time to maintaining or partnering with your agency to maintain your social media presence?

7. Do we have the resources to keep this up, or will this be a short campaign?

Similarly, unless you specify that what you're doing has a limited duration (such as a Twitter feed based on a particular event), people will expect you to keep it up. Have you budgeted the resources to continue your social media activity beyond the fiscal year?

8. How does engaging users via social media integrate into our overall marketing/communications strategy?

None of this stuff exists in a vacuum. It has to be part of a larger marketing and communications strategy. How does social media fit into what you're trying to do in all your other channels, and how will you use those channels to support each other?

9. How do we measure success?

What constitutes failure? Are you measuring views, followers, comments, or subscribers? Or are you also taking into account "harder" metrics like admissions leads, enrollments, and referrals? What's the line between success and failure in your metrics? What happens if you don't get there?

10. What will we do less of if we're spending resources on social media?

Chances are you have limited dollars. If you spend more money on social media, you have to spend less on something else. How will your overall goals be impacted by taking money away from other forms of advertising/marketing and moving it into social media?

Design

FOR colleges and universities, smart design is the currency of credibility. It's a valuable signifier of your brand's quality.

But design is more than simply glossy photos, clever layouts and a contemporary logo. Such a narrow perspective turns design into a product rather than a strategic tool with the potential to transform a brand.

Great design is born from understanding audiences. It's shaped from insights gleaned from identifying your competition's strengths and weaknesses. And it's guided by the understanding that every piece of communication—from a billboard to a website—can be a strategic asset if it unwaveringly aligns with your brand's goals.

Design driven by data and usability provides credibility. It offers organization. It creates consistency. Anything less is simply hollow imagery and meatless sizzle.

Good design happens by design, not by accident.

Design Is Not a Commodity

WHEN thinking about how design impacts real life, some of the best advice[33] comes from Diego Rodriguez, a partner at IDEO and professor at Stanford's d. School[34]: "Stop treating design as a noun."

Rodriguez's exhortation gets to the heart of the all-too-prevalent, wrong-headed thinking about design. Design, when treated as a noun, becomes nothing more than something that's slapped on at the end to pretty things up. That's a dangerous perspective to take—especially when your institution's brand is at stake.

As a marketer, you should avoid the tendency to look at the designers on your team (or at your school's ad agency) as simply decorators—people with a mysterious aesthetic talent for making things look good. That thinking can lead you down a road you don't want to go, especially when budgets are tight. Making things look good will invariably take a back seat to making things work.

Design is a process. It's everything that goes into solving a communications problem in an innovative and beautiful way.

But the two aren't separate. To be useful, by definition, something has to be used by humans in order to solve a problem or accomplish a task. If people can't use something to do these things, then it's worthless. It's *design* that makes it possible for humans to get things done.

Design is creating beautiful solutions to human problems. Design is a process. It's everything that goes into solving a communications problem in an innovative and beautiful way. When building a website, this approach means that the strategy, information architecture, database design, and the backend code are just as much a part of the design as the visual interface of the site. When creating an online ad, the visual part of the design is just one part of a larger chain of design that encompasses the targeting strategy, the call to action, the code that processes the responses elicited by the ad, the database that collects the data, the reporting system that we use to keep track of the campaign's effectiveness, and subsequent nurture campaign. The system itself is what's "designed," not just the visual part that's out front.

If you expand your definition of design in this way and understand that innovation and real-world impact are an integral part of design, it's not hard to see how design impacts our lives every day—for better or worse.

A beautifully designed object—one that delights our aesthetic sense while allowing us to accomplish tasks because its form and function are based on a real understanding of human need—makes our lives better.

A poorly designed object—one that assaults us with inferior aesthetics and whose function is obscured by a poor understanding of how people live—makes life difficult.

Of course, real life isn't always that cut-and-dried. An object might look great and function poorly. Or it might look terrible and still be able to perform its intended functions. It's essential that you demand your communications team and partners balance and integrate both form and function to create solutions that are more than the sum of their parts.

Here are a few suggestions for ensuring that design doesn't take a back seat in your marketing efforts:

Build it into the budget

So often, good design becomes a casualty because no one budgeted for it. Work with your team or agency to determine how best to provide for it. Does it mean borrowing from another line item if the budget's already been created? Or simply allocating more for the overall budget when you first kick off the project?

Have a plan

So you've got the money for design… spend it wisely. Provide your team or agency with clear direction that illuminates the audiences, goals, needs, and challenges. This will help ensure that design is created with context. The more (useful) information you can provide, the more likely the final product will do what it was meant to do—without multiple revisions and countless back-and-forth discussions.

Understand the audience

Whether you're looking to develop a website to support your school's capital campaign or creating a mobile app to enhance your student body's on-campus experience, know who you're designing for. Through interviews, focus groups, surveys, and good old-fashioned research, you can get valuable insight into their preferences, their needs, and their perceptions. Smart design depends on that understanding.

What Does Credibility Look Like?

IT'S no secret that the best design evokes the most powerful emotions. Talented storytellers use design attributes like color, hue, form, line, type, shape, texture, size, balance, and contrast to conjure specific feelings. Like a great joke, a tearjerker of a movie, or a terrific story, design inspires us to feel happy, empathetic, motivated, and even sad. It connects on the most human level.

There is nothing that we can do about how our brains are wired. We are the way we are. Advertisers are successful when they leverage our predispositions to help brands connect in meaningful, emotional ways.

Of all the emotional responses marketers can drum-up through design, trust is the most important–specifically when it comes to student recruitment.

People make "blink" judgments about the quality of a website in one twentieth of a second—usually without a whole lot of information to support it.

Online scams, fly-by-night retail sites, and other nefarious online boogeymen have instilled a natural apprehension and distrust in the minds of web users. The less they trust the medium, the less likely they will open up to a brand in meaningful, actionable ways.

And if that weren't enough, massive competition makes it even harder to reach your audiences. This has never been truer than in higher education. There are legions of competitors—beyond just other schools—vying for people's attention. Add to that the multitasking and fragmented media consumption habits of your target audience.

And when you finally connect with students, you have the tiniest opportunity to woo them. Malcolm Gladwell's *Blink*[35] argues at length that the human mind is preconditioned to make snap judgments. Researchers from Carleton University in Ottawa, Canada discovered that people make "blink" judgments about the quality of a website in one twentieth of a second—usually without a whole lot of information to support it. Published in the journal, Behaviour and Information Technology[36], the study demonstrates that first impressions have a lasting impact.

While we all may have suspected it, this study shows that people are not only making rapid emotional decisions with limited information, but it also suggests the existence of design conventions that promote similar emotional responses. And since people like being right, the initial impression sticks with them regardless of how good or bad the rest of the experience may be.

The higher education conversion funnel is a minefield littered with hazards that can thwart even the most dedicated prospect. Time, competition, attention, cost and the unknown can all discourage a prospective student from even inquiring about your school. A lot has to happen before a prospect sees your landing page. If you launch a creative campaign with compelling creative and clear calls to action across a sea of digital and traditional media venues with the precise targeting strategy and have the financial planning in place to support the right level of impressions and repetition…you should get three to six people out of a thousand who will click on your ad. Those people will be taken to a landing page. You'll then have a twentieth of a second to make the right emotional connection. How do you like those odds?

In the end, the only feeling that will advance those three to six people to the next step in the conversion funnel is trust. Trust trumps all. And since aesthetics is a dimension of trust, every marketer should strive for "trust design."

So, how do we take these lessons—and everything else we know about marketing, communications, and preferences—and create design that leads consumers a step further down the conversion funnel?

Here are a few ideas and tips that should help inspire trust… and hopefully capitalize on those hard-earned eyeballs:

Date and then marry

Having a long form on your landing page is like asking for a kiss right after meeting someone for the first time. You have to let them get to know you first. And let them initiate the transaction. Don't hit prospects with a form right away, let them ask for it with a clearly marked call-to-action. This technique can boost performance up to 60%[37].

Use simple language

People don't read online, they skim. You have a very small opportunity to connect with users, make your headline copy count. Get to the point quickly and be compelling, but not cute.

Quotes and testimonials

Benefit from social credibility. Let other people sing your praises in the form of quotes and testimonials. The number of comments, likes, and followers you have also play a part in how you're perceived, for better or worse.

Logos and credentials

Similarly, showcase logos that have high credibility, such as your own. Displaying logos of well-respected partners (remember Intel Inside?) or standard security services like VeriSign also elevates trust in a design.

Follow web conventions

People have certain expectations about how websites look and work. Follow these conventions because the alternative will raise a lot of unnecessary questions. And as users are busy guessing the answers to those questions they are not thinking about your content or offer. If you've got an underlined piece of text, users will expect that it's a link. If there's a button, users will expect that clicking it will cause something to happen. Anything that goes against standard web conventions will not only make your site difficult for users to maneuver—it'll annoy them... and annoyance is probably not a brand attribute worth protecting.

Aesthetics

A professional design that illustrates exceptional control of website design and function goes a long way. Don't skimp on design. A good-looking design *works* better than a bad looking one. Look into the Usability-Aesthetics Effect[38] if you don't believe it.

Tip-top usability

Clearly marked form labels, data input hints, error prevention and error recovery, mobile/tablet aware interfaces, and legibility are some of the many usability principles that ought to be followed to inspire trust and credibility.

Driving Action with Design

OK, so we can all agree that great design draws out specific feelings from audiences—and that trust is the most important for marketers to establish... and quickly. But what do you do with a user once you've established trust through design? How do you capitalize on that trust and drive them to action?

There are plenty of formulas[39] and frameworks[40] out there that purport to drive conversion and results. Some are complex and some are simple.

Not to suggest that design is the answer to every problem, but in this case, it is at least a partial answer. Content and transaction completes the picture.

After decades of doing this stuff, we've crafted this three-track model to drive action. It's a simple way to squeeze higher yields from the traffic generated in online marketing campaigns, and it's helped to improve conversions from 50% to 70% and higher on the same traffic. We call it **Action-Driven Design.**

It exploits the power of a strong (and relevant) offer expressed through the most effective **design, content and transaction** techniques.

People spend 80% of their time reading what's "above the fold," and 20% on what's below it.[41]

Content

Face it. People don't read much online[42]. If you're lucky, they'll read a headline and a photo caption. You have an extremely small window to connect, intrigue and drive action[43]. Focused, simple, authentic, pithy and surprising copy that directly connects with the user[44] has the best chance of being read.

In many campaigns, we employ more than 20 landing pages to effectively market to various audience segments. All in all, our landing pages are simple and concise. Calls to action are obvious, big, and clear. And of course, all of the content on these landing pages is optimized accordingly to support the search engine optimization strategy.

Face it. People don't read much online. If you're lucky, they'll read a headline and a photo caption.

What Part of a Web Page Do Visitors Pay the Most Attention to?

Based on the percentage of time visitors spent viewing the screen above and below "the fold."

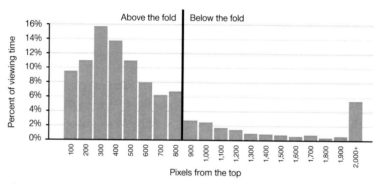

Source: useit.com

Design

Get ready, here come the acronyms, starting with CATCH, a concept that guides landing page design. It symbolizes the most important user interface and graphic design principles for driving action:

- Credibility of messaging and sources[45]. Consider including powerful statistics about alumni employment rates or testimonials from famous graduates;
- Aesthetic-usability effect to enhance perception of value[46]. Professional photography and sophisticated design elements such as border, headers, and backgrounds make a huge difference;
- Typography that's legible and logically arranged[47]. The higher the contrast between the type and the background, the better;

- Chunking content together into logical sections to aid comprehension and recall[48]; and
- Hierarchy to organize information for easier access and scanability[49]. Use section titles and headlines to give the user a good idea of what the page is about, even if they don't read through all of the body copy.

Transaction

Use the PACED concept to guide the usability or transactional dimension on your landing pages. The acronym is meant to focus design on the most important usability principles that drive action:

- **Progressive disclosure** shows information when it's most appropriate[50]. For example, rather than display a huge list of links in a menu, have them hidden until a user hovers over the menu or clicks on it;
- **Affordance** ensures that the page functions act as users expect it should[51]. If there's a play button in a video pane on your site, clicking on it should play a video, not open up an email message or take you to a form;
- **Conventions** of design are universally understood by users[52]. If a user needs to search your website, they'll look for the search pane in the utility navigation at the top first;
- **Error Recovery** guides users through missteps in the transaction process[53]. If they've mistyped a word in the search bar, present them with suggested correct spellings; and
- **"Date and then Marry"** calls for a connection before intimacy. Instead of presenting users immediately with a form, the page should use a button to direct them to the form. This technique has been independently proven to boost performance by up to 60%[54]. The rationalization behind this finding suggests that people are more likely to offer their personal information if it's a self-initiated task, rather than being pushed into providing the info. Not to mention, eschewing the form on the main page also simplifies the design of the page, which is always welcomed by prospects.

This isn't meant to be a *silver bullet*. Developing the perfect landing page requires a little bit of trial and error. Start with the best recommendation you can and A/B test continuously until the landing pages are fully optimized.

Like most things in life, the more you put into it, the more you will get out of it.

Should We Redesign Our Website?

TO some, design is a verb that describes the process leading to the creation of something in order to produce a desired outcome. To others design is a noun, usually describing visual qualities. To the more artistically minded, design might simply be a way of talking about what something looks like. And to the mechanically or architecturally oriented person, design might include both the visual and functional aspects of a product, a building, or a piece of software. If we didn't put you to sleep in the Design chapter, you know where we stand on this.

Regardless, everyone has their own view on this topic. Over the past decade, the working definition of design and how it applies to business has continued to expand.

What's the economic benefit of design?

Does this new emphasis on design have economic benefits? Is it possible to link design to profit? The answer seems to be yes.

One of the most compelling studies on how design impacts the bottom line is "The Impact of Design on Stock Market Performance"[55] published by the Design Council in the UK. They examined a portfolio of 63 companies traded on the UK FTSE between 1994 and 2003. Their methodology didn't strive for an exact definition of design, but rather chose public companies that had been the recipients of prestigious design awards. Their study found that companies who emphasized design (however it was defined) outperformed the FTSE 100 index by 200% during the time of the study!

How does design impact the performance of a website?

We know that aesthetics can influence whether or not users are able to successfully complete tasks (see Don Norman and his work in "Emotion & Design: Attractive Things Work Better"[56]). Successful task completion is obviously important for any website, but when the tasks to be completed are those that generate revenue—such as purchasing something or applying to a college—aesthetics really start to have a direct economic impact.

It also turns out that the impact of design on user opinion happens incredibly quickly. We alluded to a study in our chapter on credibility, noting the researchers at Carleton University's Human Oriented (HOT) Lab[57] who flashed websites on a screen in front of a group of volunteers and then recorded their impressions of the websites[58]. While this might not seem all that innovative or groundbreaking, it is interesting because the sites were flashed on the screen for a mere 50 milliseconds. They found that the impressions formed by subjects who only saw the site for 1/20th of a second were pretty much the same as those who had more time to study the page. In other words, all it takes is 1/20th of a second for a person to form an opinion (good or bad) of your site! Even more importantly, the researchers found that the impression formed in that 1/20th of a second had a halo effect that colored users' impressions of the site, even when they had the opportunity to explore it. If they liked it during that split-second glance, they tended to continue to like it as they used it and thus tended to use the site more.

But is it worth redesigning an underperforming site?

A Forrester Research study[59] on the ROI of website redesign seems to suggest that redesigning an underperforming website is worth the effort:

- 97% of businesses surveyed failed basic usability standards;
- Among the companies surveyed, redesign projects increased site traffic as much as 15%;
- Amazingly, conversion rates increased between 20-50% from a pre-redesign average of 1.5%; and
- Service calls were reduced in volume by as much as 20,000 calls.

Overall, Forrester estimates the return on investment for redesigning a site to be 70-500%. Even for smaller sites, the effect still holds. They found that while larger efforts produced more in total dollars, small projects still showed positive ROI and produced higher overall relative returns.

Forrester estimates the return on investment for redesigning a site to be 70-500%.

There is a lot that can be done to make advertising landing pages, mobile sites and micro-sites more aesthetically pleasing (and effective). But measuring the ROI of such changes can be tough. Design quality is somewhat subjective and can be difficult to measure. It can also be difficult to measure the performance of a site unless everyone has agreed on the purpose of the site and the metric(s) that will be used to measure success. In order to address these issues, we usually recommend measuring something that everyone can agree on: the marginal difference.

Measuring the marginal difference

Your agency of record should be able to tell you how your school's website or advertising campaign is performing. That's your baseline. Then, introduce a design change and measure the change in performance. That performance boost has an economic value that can be traced back to the design change. And suddenly, you have a metric that everyone can appreciate.

This much is true: design matters. Make every dollar count and every pixel earn its keep.

Of course, all of this theory doesn't mean much if you can't get the ball rolling. Here are some things to consider before tackling a website redesign in earnest:

Listen to your audience

This should be as much a discussion of functionality as it is a discussion of design. Survey a full spectrum of users from across the university for input on how the site's being used, what's working, what's not, and what elements it should include to better meet their needs. From online and email surveys to in-depth focus groups and in-person interviews, you've got a range of tools to tap into those opinions. We recommend employing multiple tactics to ensure that you reach the widest variety of respondents.

Look at your data

Also be prepared to dig into the web analytics of the current site. They'll provide powerful insight into not only how visitors use your site (e.g. popular pages, user paths, and time on site) but also how they got there (e.g. referral sources and search keywords) and why they left (e.g. exit pages and bounce rates).

Be a spy

It never hurts to peek over the hedge at what other schools are doing. It'll not only provide you with ideas for improvements, but cautionary tales as well. Look at somone else's design? Does it fit their brand? Is the site easy to use? How are they speaking to audiences? How are they organizing content? Are they using a similar content management system? Do they have functional aspects that seem to work well? Is there anything on the site that makes you absolutely jealous? Or anything that makes you thankful you don't work there?

Get buy-in

Even smaller colleges have a lot of moving parts at the top—and that means a lot of people who have to weigh-in on an initiative before it gets the green light. Expect this to be a Herculean task. But it'll be less so if you aren't going it alone. Solicit the support of key influencers throughout your institution—especially student representatives, faculty, executive staff, alumni organization staff, and marketing folks. A redesign is a major undertaking. You're going to need allies.

Making Your Website Play Nice on Any Device

RESPONSIVE web design is all the rage these days, considering it was only a few short years ago, Ethan Marcotte[60] conceived the term. Much like when Jeffrey Zeldman[61] coined "web standards" and Jesse James Garrett[62] came up with Ajax[63], Ethan gave us common definitions that unified techniques and standards some of us had been using all along.

The coining and popularization of these terms each birthed a new round of innovation, creativity and standards in web design. And for that, both users and creators are eternally grateful.

What's responsive design?

Before we get much further, perhaps it might be a good idea to define responsive design for the 90% of people out there who (thankfully!) may go their whole lives without ever having to lament over terms like "single source design" and "fluid grids."

In the simplest sense, responsive design is the use of design and development techniques to make sure content displays and functions correctly on any screen—from gargantuan desktop monitors to squint-inducing smartphone screens. In responsive design, the designers and developers work closely to make content work across varying resolutions.

The technique uses fluid grids, flexible images, flexible type and

In the simplest sense, responsive design is the use of design and development techniques to make sure content displays and functions correctly on any screen.

media queries to deliver resolution-appropriate designs to end-users. A single website is designed and built to adjust itself according to the accessing device's screen size to provide the best possible experience.

So, should a website be responsive?

It's become the question du jour in web design and development. Logically, the right answer is "No." But emotionally, the answer is "yes," "no," and "maybe."

In other words, "it depends."

We know it doesn't sound like much of an answer, but it is the right one. In the end, the decision should be driven by a number of interconnected factors such as:

- Business objective;
- Target audience;
- Creative direction; and
- Cost of ownership.

From a business point of view (the cost of making and owning a website), it allows managers to benefit: they only shell out cash for one site that's capable of being delivered over multiple platforms and resolutions. There is an undeniable economic value of single source design, production, and content because managing one website takes less time than managing two or three or… well, you get the idea.

Responsive design is interesting because it introduces "the business of interactive" as a major factor in the decision making process. Not to say that the "business" dimension was always absent, but recognizing it is now a **major** consideration. But there are other factors—many more, actually. Besides the economics of it (which is sometimes enough to win a client's support), there's also the usability, content, information architecture, design, and conventions to consider.

The pros and cons of responsive design

Not surprisingly, the popularization of responsive design has stirred up a lot of discussion (read: rabid disagreement) on this topic.

In one camp is famed usability guru Jakob Nielsen who asserts[64] that "it's cheap but degrading to reuse content and design across diverging media forms like print vs. online or desktop vs. mobile. Superior UX (user experience) requires tight platform integration." We agree with most of his conclusions, but we're not about to give him the final word.

Why? Well, Jakob, there's the simple matter of the tried-and-true 80/20 rule[65]. Twenty percent of the functionality will be used by 80% of the users. In a perfect world, with all the time and money, superior UX is always the right answer. In the real world, where people with real budgets and time pressures live, his approach in unrealistic.

In fact, with the use of mobile Internet doubling every year since 2009, with 1.03 billion worldwide smartphone owners in 2011[66], and with mobile web searches scheduled to surpass desktop searches by 2013[67], it seems like a very good argument could be made to make *all web design* responsive to some extent.

Nothing is perfect. If you decide to implement a responsive design, make sure you plan it out. There are certain things everyone should know about and avoid[68]. Probably one of the most interesting perspectives is how responsive design could change the development process. We've had some lively and colorful (and always healthy) discussions about this. While we've delivered award-winning responsive designs[69], we are—much like everyone else—still refining our process and approach.

Here are some questions to help guide your decision to use responsive design or not:

1. What is the mobile traffic coming to our site over the last 12 months and what percent growth is that year-over-year?
2. What is your institutional policy for mobile experiences?
3. Is your organization technically, creatively, and emotionally (yes, emotionally) ready for responsive design?
4. Are there particular reasons why a separate mobile-only website makes more sense? Examples include super-long content that needs to be rewritten or completely excluded from mobile consumption or an information architecture that needs to be streamlined for mobile delivery.
5. Is the person or team responsible for managing content ready and capable of managing multiple websites—or do they only have the capacity for the one site? This is less of an issue for smaller websites.
6. What specific user experiences can be delivered through a mobile only implementation? Can they also be done through

responsive design?

7. Do you have the time, budget and institutional support for a desktop site as well as a dedicated mobile site?

One final caveat: regardless of what you end up doing, test your work. Not just for usability testing, which is extremely important, but also for functionality and rendering. Suddenly, there are *many* screen sizes to accommodate and it seems that the number of varied size devices gets bigger every time you look. Whether you decide to launch a responsive design or not, one thing is clear: The decision is not an easy one and it requires serious consideration.

How to Keep Your Mobile Site from Sucking

WE'RE sure, over the last few years, your marketing team has had more than a few arguments about whether or not you should produce an app or whether you should just "mobilize" your website via CSS, a process made a lot easier with most modern content management systems.

For a while now, the answer seemed to be the ever-popular "it depends." If you wanted something simple (e.g. a calculator, access to your website) creating a mobile site seemed

But do most schools actually need apps? The answer: probably not.

like the way to go. On the other hand, if you wanted to do something highly interactive (such as a game), an app seemed like the way to go. Besides—be honest with yourself, now—saying you had an app seemed a lot cooler than saying that you reformatted your website.

But do most schools actually need apps? The answer: probably not. It may be time to swallow your pride and take the more economical route of going with a mobile site, especially now with the explosion of new tools and techniques such as responsive design that make it a lot easier to create an app-like experience on your mobile site. Heck, Chrome has a browser-based version of Angry Birds[70]. This is real, people.

There's no question that people like to make apps: Apple's App Store now has more than 650,000 apps[71] (and counting), and the pace of app creation doesn't appear to be slowing down.

But lots of folks are going mobile with their websites, too. And this makes sense considering that by 2015 experts expect that nearly 9 in 10 people on earth[72] will have a mobile phone. And while schools are scrambling to take their sites to the mobile web, there's only one problem: Most of those will probably suck. Big time.

Harsh? We don't think so. Most of these mobile sites are simply reformatted versions of desktop websites.

You know you've seen them: Mobile sites that don't take into account simple truths, such as the fact that people use their fingers to navigate and that entering data is tough with a tiny on-screen keyboard. Other mobile sins include text that's too long, problematic navigation widgets, images that take up too much of the screen, and too many menu choices.

But as we poise ourselves for the inevitable onslaught of mobile sites, we have to face bigger issues than just formatting and usability quirks. We've got to rethink the very nature of the website in the mobile age if we're going to avoid this suckage.

First, let's consider the most common consumer mobile platform activities[73]. What do people like to do? Download stuff to make their phones more fun (ringtones, graphics, games), keep in touch via social networking, entertain themselves with audio and video, manage their money, and find stuff with location-based services. If you think about your own mobile behavior, you'll probably see a lot of your own activities in that list.

What won't you find? Reading long scrolling pages of marketing copy; filling out complicated forms; learning your school's history; browsing lists of your administrative staff; downloading PDFs. In short, you won't find them doing a lot of the things that many schools offer on their desktop websites.

More than half of smartphone users actually prefer their smartphone over their computer when accessing the Internet.

If you dig a little deeper into consumer behavior on wireless devices, things get even more interesting. A survey[74] from Prosper Mobile Insights found that eight out of ten smartphone users used their phones to look for products and services while on-the-go. They also used their phones during their shopping to read reviews, scan QR codes for more info, and perform other product research. Interestingly, more than half of smartphone users actually prefer their smartphone over their computer when accessing the Internet—another indicator that mobile web access is going to be even more important for marketers in the future.

But what are tablet users doing? Well, 75% of them are using iPads, according to iPass[75]. The same report also found that 34% of "mobile workers" who don't have a tablet plan to get one in the next six months. And what do they want to use it for? Note taking, contact management, office suites, social media, and web conferencing topped the list.

Tablet users (and smartphone users, too) also tend to make the devices a part of their lives, using them in situations where they previously probably wouldn't have thought of using a computer. A 2011 study by Nielsen[76] found that high numbers of tablet users reported using their tablets while watching TV, lying in bed, hanging out with friends and family, in the bathroom, and the always-popular "waiting for something."

We can't dismiss it: The mobile web is different animal than "traditional" web. If you're going to create a successful mobile presence, you need to understand what those differences are:

Context matters

It's not just who your users are, but where they are when they access your mobile offerings—and who they're with.

They've got short attention spans

They're bored and waiting in line. They're getting jostled on the train during their commute. Requiring them to focus for more than a minute or so isn't going to fly.

They're trying to solve problems that people on-the-go need to solve

They need directions. They're trying to find a friend. They're in a new city and they're hungry and they're looking for food that reminds them of home. They're in the school bookstore and can't remember the required book they need or the class they need it for. They need solutions, not exposition.

They're trying to connect to other people

Mobile social networking apps are popular for the same reason mobile phones are popular: people want to connect with other people. Make it easy to connect to your school and its various communities via your mobile site using the built-in social or location-aware capabilities of the phone.

They're all thumbs

On-the-go data entry isn't easy. Don't require prospective students to fill out complicated data acquisition forms or navigate tiny text links. If you must gather textual information, make it short and sweet.

They're not using computers

This is an obvious one, but it's one that many people seem to forget: a phone is *not* a teeny-tiny laptop (and a tablet isn't a laptop without a keyboard). Leverage the unique abilities of the device your customers are using to access your site. How can you use the camera? Can you let them record and submit audio? What about VOIP chat? Can you utilize knowledge of their location to help them solve the problem they came to your site for in the first place?

Screen real estate is sacred

Sure, you may have a killer infographic or a map that looks great on a laptop, but on a smartphone screen, people are going to have to scroll around to see the whole thing. Chances are by the time they get to the bottom they'll have forgotten what they're looking at. Ditto for menus and text. Keep it simple and keep it on as few screens as possible.

Less is more

If your computer-based website and your mobile site are the same thing (only formatted differently), you're doing something wrong. Your mobile site should be a subset of your main website. It should focus only on the kinds of information and features mobile users need. Pare down mercilessly. Put yourself in the shoes of your mobile customers: Was there ever a time you were on-the-go that you desperately needed to read a motivational message from the president of the university or watch student testimonials?

We didn't think so.

Media and Channels

IT used to be that it would be enough that an institution looking to boost enrollment could film a few commercials, record a couple radio spots, run a few ads in magazines and newspapers, slap up a billboard, and maybe even buy a few display ads on the web (if they were feeling particularly cutting edge that cycle). It was a simpler time.

And for University X, not much has changed. It still places the same ads in the same places using a paint-by-numbers approach to media that hasn't changed much over the last few decades. Unfortunately for University X, that's not only ineffective, it's downright dangerous.

The media market has always evolved. From town criers to newspapers to radio to TV to web to mobile, and everything else in between, media choices have always been evolving. But rather than a smooth, gradual evolution, it's been more like a snowball rolling down a mountain. It starts small and slow. But then it picks up speed. It gets bigger and faster the further down the mountain it gets. The difference is, in media, there's no bottom of the mountain in sight; just endless possibilities stretching out into infinity.

Or, if you're University X, never ending fear. It's not that University X marketers don't want to be relevant, successful, or even heroic. They do. But they're afraid. They avoid risk. They like the way things have always been done. Rather than take risks, they're likely to pull the emergency brake anytime they're encouraged to venture outside their comfort zone. They're unwilling to try new media (or new approaches to old media) for fear that they'll get left holding the bag if the campaign bombs.

We get it. In fact, most agencies get it. The only problem is that few are able or willing to walk their clients through the fire. They don't make the effort—or don't have the knowledge—to provide their clients with the knowledge, the understanding, and the confidence they need to break out of the "same old-same old" trap.

All the more reason why agencies and institutions must build strong relationships based on honesty, trust, and understanding. Each side needs to know what the other's pain points, limitations, and deal-breakers are. We've found the clients who get the best results are the ones who not only trust us, but whom we trust, too. It's not a vendor-client transaction. It's a relationship of equals dedicated to a mutual goal.

In this section you'll find insights from the cutting-edge of media and learn about everything from which channels are the most underrated to which bits of conventional wisdom are more like mythology.

Whether it's surfing the bleeding edge or speaking to core truths of marketing, you can be assured that what you read here has been harvested through real-life experience—experiences which could have only been had by working with some very understanding, trusting partners.

When the Metrics Don't Match the Media

WHAT'S the click-through rate (CTR) on your latest TV campaign? What's the bounce rate on your radio spots? How many "likes" did your print ad get?

Why are these absurd questions? It's because the metrics don't match the media, right?

So why is the marketing industry still judging social and mobile advertising by the same metrics we use to measure online display or search advertising?

In a time when more and more marketing budgets are being moved into digital, this isn't a trivial question. If we're going to be spending money, we need to know if a channel is working. It's impossible to know if it's working if we're not measuring the right things. And the place where marketers (and everyone else) seem to be missing the mark the most when it comes to metrics is social media…Facebook in particular.

Facebook took a lot of heat, especially after its disappointing IPO. And those hits weren't only to the stock prices. The BBC made a big splash by revealing[77] the results of an experiment it conducted to find out the commercial value of consumer "likes" on the social networking service. The article's bottom line: "Companies are wasting large sums of money on adverts to gain 'likes' from Facebook members who have no real interest in their products," a conclusion reached after discovering that many "likes" come from people who aren't in the target market of the advertiser or from scammers, spammers, and fake profiles.

To be fair, the BBC followed up with a Q&A session[78] with a Facebook spokesperson who was quick to point out just how great an advertising platform Facebook can be due to its huge audience and global reach (surprise!). Mr. Spokesperson also quibbled with the BBC's "experiment"—a page for a fake bagel shop—and the BBC's use of the "likes" metric with a local company on a global medium. "In the real world," opined Mr. Spokesperson, "if you hand out flyers for a pizza restaurant in Birmingham to people in Beijing and Mexico City, then you're not going to get the customers you want. The same applies to online advertising."

Not to sound too British, but yes, indeed. Using "likes" coming in from all over the globe as a metric for judging the effectiveness of a locally-focused Facebook ad *is* a little silly. Unless the aforementioned pizza restaurant in Birmingham has a worldwide reputation among customers rich enough to fly thousands of miles for a slice, worrying about "likes" from Mumbai doesn't make a lot of sense. Yet that's exactly what we do as an industry when judging the effectiveness of Facebook advertising. A recent poll[79] by Reuters found that "four out of five Facebook, Inc. users have never bought a product or service as a result of advertising or comments on the social network site," leading it to conclude that "much more needs to be done to turn its…customer base [of more than one billion] into advertising dollars."

> **85% of social media-using respondents rarely or never clicked on a Facebook ad.**

Another poll[80] conducted by the AP and CNBC before Facebook's IPO revealed that 85% of social media-using respondents rarely or never clicked on a Facebook ad[81] and that 54% "would not feel safe purchasing goods and services like clothing or travel on Facebook." If that weren't bad enough, only 18% of respondents had "deep confidence" in CEO Marc Zuckerberg's ability to run the company, though it added a ray of hope by adding that 51% of respondents who had seen *The Social Network* had a "favorable impression" of the young mogul.

All issues of bias aside (Reuters, AP, and CNBC *are* competitors of Facebook, after all), these measures of consumer behavior seem to match previous findings by outside analysts, even if they may have their own potential axes to grind. A May 2012 study[82] by search marketing firm WordStream, for example, found that click-through rates for Facebook ads (0.051%) were blown away by the CTR of Google search ads (0.4%). Facebook ads even lagged the average CTR of ads across the web (0.1%). Another study[83] by e-commerce consultants Monetate found that search was far more effective than either email or social media for driving traffic to e-commerce sites. While search drove 29.67% of inbound traffic, email drove a paltry 6.58% and social a mere 2.15%.

Internet Ad Clickthrough Rate
A Quick Comparison

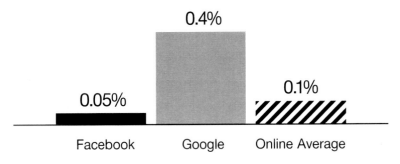

Source: WordStream

It would seem that in the face of numbers like this, marketers would be thinking twice about spending money on social, right? After all, recent predictions[84] indicate that spending on social media advertising will grow from the $3.8 billion in 2011 to almost $10 billion by 2016.

Maybe marketers would worry if they actually had a strategy for using social media or were even sure about how to measure its effectiveness. Unfortunately, as eConsultancy's "State of Social 2011" report[85] revealed, two out of five companies can't put an ROI on their social media spending. In fact, only one out of five companies were even able to calculate the ROI for half the money they were putting into social media. For two out of three companies surveyed, the best they could do was point to an increase in traffic to their corporate websites as a measure of success for their social media campaigns. Another study by eConsultancy earlier in the year was even more depressing when it came to indicating any level of sophistication with social marketing: 91%

As marketers, we seem to have developed a kind of social media schizophrenia. We tell our clients (or bosses) that social media is important because it will allow us to "engage with our customers" and "build brand awareness among our target markets," yet we want to measure our success with simple metrics like click-throughs and "likes" and hits on our home pages.

of marketers surveyed reported that traffic volume was an important metric. And Engagement? Or brand awareness? Yeah…they trailed way behind.

As marketers, we seem to have developed a kind of social media schizophrenia. We tell our clients (or bosses) that social media is important because it will allow us to "engage with our customers" and "build brand awareness among our target markets," yet we want to measure our success with simple metrics like click-throughs and "likes" and hits on our home pages.

So is all this social media stuff nothing more than high-minded hype destined to do nothing more than add a few more squares to our Buzzword Bingo[86] cards? Is social marketing just smoke and mirrors? Does the emperor truly have no clothes?

Maybe not. Maybe the failure of Facebook advertising indicated in the studies isn't a failure of the platform but of what we're measuring and what we expect social media to do. To illustrate this[87], ad agency MDG identified four different advertising goals: lead generation, brand awareness, driving people to local businesses, and encouraging consumers to interact with brands. It then collated a number of different studies in order to compare the value of search and the value of social in achieving each outcome.

Not surprisingly, the bottom line is you need both! As it turns out, search is better for lead generation and local business visibility while social rules when it comes to driving brand awareness and interactivity. We all win!

All cheap sarcasm aside, there's something profound here when you look beneath the surface and think about *why* these numbers are what they are. The answer is pretty surprising.

Lead generation and local business visibility (the search winners) are highly measurable, linear, consumer-directed behaviors. Leads are generated when students are considering which college is right for them—and actively reach out for more information.

On the other hand, brand awareness and interactivity are a lot "squishier" and don't lend themselves as well to simple measurements. They're less about hard numbers and more about attitudes and feelings that eventually drive consumer behavior. Search is a narrow activity we engage in when we're trying to find something or solve a problem, while social is more about casting a wide net, interacting with our friends, and talking about our problems or needs. Seen in this light, search and social are two different behaviors that consumers engage in for different reasons. They're not the same…so why should they be measured in the same way?

One way to think about media choices in a more abstract sense is to think about their characteristics in terms of something we all have plenty of experience with: food. Consuming mass media, for example, is like being fed: it's a passive activity where we cede control to the programmers. Because it's a passive activity, it's good for telling people what to do, influencing attitudes and opinions by feeding them directly to consumers.

On the other hand, search is a lot more like preparing a meal and feeding ourselves. It's a controlled activity directed toward a goal (dinner) and proceeds in more or less linear steps. To market to people who are cooking their metaphorical dinners, the trick is to do what search does best: Insert your messages into the process and help people find the information and ingredients they want.

Search is a narrow activity we engage in when we're trying to find something or solve a problem, while social is more about casting a wide net, interacting with our friends, and talking about our problems or needs.

And social? Well, social's a big potluck party with tons of different grub heaped on tables prepared by our friends. It's just waiting to be grazed and gobbled up as we see fit. In this kind of setting nobody wants a pushy host demanding that they try certain things. Social is about hanging out, chatting each other up, and sampling the nifty new things that others have brought to the table. Maybe we'll ask a friend for a recipe if we like a particular dish, but we want that decision to be our own.

We could torture this metaphor even more, but you get the point. Different media provide consumers with different things and offer different opportunities for marketers that depend on the different characteristics inherent in each particular medium. And because these channels are different, we should use different kinds of metrics to measure, different ways to evaluate their effectiveness. If we want to know where to advertise and how to measure if our advertising is working or not, we have to measure the right thing and expect the right results.

The bottom line?

All ads are not created equal. Nor should they be. To accurately understand where to spend your marketing dollars, you have to understand what you're trying to accomplish, how to measure its effectiveness, and, above all, why one channel is better than another for what you're trying to do. Anything less and you're stuck with justifying your TV campaigns by measuring their click-through rates.

And that's just silly.

The Great Click Debate

SEX, religion, and politics. Macs vs. PCs. There are some topics that most of us avoid talking about in polite company. And if you're in online marketing, there's another topic that you probably avoid, too: whether or not clicks matter.

The Great Click Debate has been raging pretty much since HotWired posted the first banner ad[88] way back in October 1994 that asked the question "Have you ever clicked your mouse right here?" and answered it with a bold "You will!"

Clicks were the great promise of online media. While traditional advertising could only be measured by sampling, surveys, and other guestimation methods, online advertising was sold as being completely accountable. Gone were the days that made department store mogul and unofficial father of modern advertising, John Wanamaker, complain, "Half my advertising is wasted...I just don't know which half." With the click you were going to know *exactly* what part of your advertising was wasted.

It didn't take long, however, for the promise of directly-measurable online advertising to fade. Publishers and ad folks who were used to being able to finesse the value of the campaigns they were running in traditional media were suddenly confronted with—GASP!—having to account for why the ads they were selling their clients weren't working. Icky terms like "ROI" started to creep into uncomfortable conversations with clients who wanted to know why nobody was clicking on their ads.

The industry soon responded by working hard to convince their clients that, even if people weren't clicking, they were still being exposed to the brand, by golly, that had value! In 1997, the Interactive Advertising Bureau released a study[69] that said that online ads were effective even if people weren't clicking on them. And thus the Great Click Debate began.

Like so many great debates, the "clicks vs. branding" debate is often fought with "facts" generated by people with a stake in one side or the other. Obviously, the IAB study mentioned above has a bias because it comes from the industry group whose sole purpose is to sell online advertising! Groups like Nielsen have been pushing for a "GRP-like" system of measuring[90] online advertising that ditches clicks for exposure. Digital agency Eyeblaster suggest Dwell[91] as a metric to replace the click, arguing that the amount of time a user spends viewing or interacting with an ad is a better metric than whether or not they click through it to another site.

New technologies have added to the debate. While various social media formats provide somewhat traditional display advertising models in one form or another, clicks have been overtaken by measures of social engagement[92], which seeks to couple brand awareness with social media activities around the brand. Not to be outdone, mobile media also is being touted as the great brander, with some studies[93] finding that "mobile ad campaigns are five times more effective" than traditional online ad units.

Of course, the other side (read Google, Facebook, and other CPC and CPA properties) has risen to fame and fortune *because of* clicks. They've embraced the direct-response model whole-heartedly and have been embraced by everyone from big CPG advertisers to mom and pop businesses around the globe. Their self-service offerings that combine high levels of accountability with the efficiency of only paying for what you need have appealed to the long tail of niche advertisers and those with hard-to-reach target audiences and limited budgets.

Clicks have been overtaken by measures of social engagement, which seeks to couple brand awareness with social media activities around the brand.

So, who's right? Well, we'd like to settle the Great Click Debate once and for all so we'll just come out and say it: they both are.

A cop out? No, the truth.

See, the Great Click Debate is a lot like the Great Mac vs. PC debate. Zealots exist on both sides, fighting a holy war over details that matter to nobody except them. To right-click or not? Should clicking an "X" quit a program or just close a window? Whatever. It doesn't matter. What really should matter is whether or not you're using the right tool for the job that's in front of you. PCs are better at some things. So are Macs. It just depends on what you want to do and what you're comfortable with. Arguing the point is idiotic.

The same goes for clicks vs. brand exposure/dwell time/whatever. Choosing the right metric to measure the effectiveness of your campaign isn't a matter of holy doctrine but rather should be based on *what you're actually trying to accomplish*.

Identify your purpose, and pick a media for it

For brand awareness, use a format that's better for building brand awareness. More likely than not, that's going to be a format that's large, bold, and can contain video, animation, or allow for interactivity...in short, a display ad format. If you're trying to drive response, use tools and techniques that drive response: attention-grabbing display advertising that invites clicks (ahem...dancing mortgage ads) or place yourself in front of the consumer who's looking to solve a problem or answer a question.

Use the appropriate measure for your goals

That means that if you're going to be running a branding campaign, you should measure your success by brand awareness measures, not how many clicks the ad gets! On the other hand, if you're trying to drive leads (clicks or other actions that take the consumer to a website or landing page), then for gosh sakes measure leads...but don't expect that you're going to move the awareness needle too much. You might (Facebook ads seem to be good at doing this because of their size and target-ability), but that's not what you're being measured on. If you want clicks, count clicks!

Set expectations

So perhaps this isn't an either/or proposition between awareness and action. After all, brand-response marketing says you can do both[94]. But even though it sounds simple, it's awfully hard to realize in the real world where directors, VPs, and chief muckity-mucks seem to want both. Setting expectations with them from the beginning (clicks or branding), buying media that matches your goals (display ads or CPC text ads), and reminding them throughout the campaign about what you were being paid to measure (response or awareness) can help you mitigate misunderstandings and misconceptions. In the end, you've got to deliver what you promised, but at least everyone will know what that is.

TV Is Dead! Long Live TV!

DOES the impending death of a small TV startup mark the beginning of the end for TV?

In February 2012, four-year-old Canoe Ventures announced[95] that it was laying off 120 employees and shifting the final 30-or-so employees to concentrate on video on demand. The company, created by cable giants Comcast, Cox, Time Warner, Charter Communications, Cablevision, and Bright House had promised to "reimagine" the television experience by allowing viewers to request information by mail from advertisers by pushing a button on their remote controls. They'd also hoped to allow cable networks to target ads down to the neighborhood level, but scrapped those plans in 2009 due to technical issues.

The issue isn't that people are going to stop watching video content any time soon, but rather that how they watch it is in the midst of a radical change as big as the change faced by the music and film industries.

It would seem on the surface that the shuttering of such a relatively small company wouldn't be that big of a deal to anyone except the employees affected and maybe industry insiders, but Canoe's capsizing may be the canary in the cable TV coal mine that augers something much bigger. Why? Because if some of the biggest TV companies in the world couldn't get advertisers jazzed about the future of TV, then TV as we know it may have no future.

Before you get out the butterfly net and drag us to the loony bin, note that we said "TV as we know it." The issue isn't that people are going to stop watching video content any time soon, but rather that *how* they watch it is in the midst of a radical change as big as the change faced by the music and film industries.

The signs are unmistakable. According to comScore's recent "2012 Digital Future in Focus"[96] report, online video viewing increased 43% in 2011. In December 2011 alone, Americans watched 43.5 billion content video streams. About half of that was on YouTube, followed by Vevo, Hulu, and Netflix. That's a lot of video.

At the same time, Nielsen is reporting[97] that the number of "cord cutters" (people ditching cable to go with a combination of over-the-air and Internet content) increased nearly 23% over the past year. And while this group still watches more "traditional TV than online TV," overall cord-cutters watch half as much broadcast TV and twice as much online TV as the rest of the U.S. population.

But it might be those whom Analyst Stefan Anninger calls "cord-nevers"[98] who really show us where TV is going. "Cord-nevers" have grown up with the Internet and the content-is-free culture and believe that pay-TV is a rip-off. They're also growing up in a down economy where the average cable bill[99] is around $100. When faced with the choice of a $100 monthly bill for cable or around $20 a month for a couple of streaming video subscriptions (say Netflix and Hulu+), cutting (or never getting) "the cord" seems like a no-brainer. Just take a look at the Hulu[100] and Netflix[101] paid subscriber numbers. The trend seems to be pretty clear…even more so when you look at the demographics[102] that show that the biggest users of these services are Millennials—the core demographic for four-year college enrollment.

> **But if we want to glimpse the future of TV, the music industry probably represents the best model.**

Of course, the naysayers among you reading this may point to the fact that "cord cutters" only make up about 5% of U.S. households today. True. But it's also true that in every instance where the Internet has offered an alternative to old media, old media loses. Just take a look at newspapers[103], CDs[104], books[105], and magazines[106]. If content can be gotten cheaper, faster, easier, and with more choice, it will be.

But if we want to glimpse the future of TV, the music industry probably represents the best model. Even with all the hand-wringing going on by the Recording Industry Association of America (RIAA) about digital content and piracy, music sales have actually been going up[107] in the U.S. as a result of the explosion in digital music sales. While CDs may have gone the way of CRT TVs, music—the content contained on CDs, the stuff we actually care about—still continues to sell at a rapid clip. The Internet has separated the content (music) from its former means of distribution (shiny plastic discs sold in quaintly-named record stores). Content and container have been irrevocably separated.

That's why the demise of Canoe that we mentioned at the beginning of this segment is so important. It's not that people don't want to watch and interact with video content, it's just that they don't want to do it in a format that seems increasingly inconvenient given the new choices they have. Why would a consumer want to wait for information about a product to be sent to them by mail when they can just go online and find it in seconds? If the record-breaking social numbers racked up during the Grammy Awards are any indication[108], the digital omnivores[109] of today want their interaction *now*.

So is TV dead? If by TV, we mean the traditional broadcast-sit-down-and-watch-one-screen-with-the-family model then, yes, the Reaper's sharpening his scythe. But if we broaden the definition of TV to include any commercially-supported video content, then the future is pretty bright. As advertisers, we just need to get over the fact that the old model is on the way out. Start looking to a future where all TV will be interactive, online, and watched whenever and wherever viewers want to watch it.

Of course, this has an impact on higher education marketers who are faced with challenging budgets and ever-increasing expectations to hit enrollment and funding goals.

You *can* track TV

While easier said than done, it is possible to measure the success of traditional TV advertising—though it won't be perfect. For ads driving viewers to your website, consider taking a page from the direct marketer's playbook: use URLs or landing pages specific to that particular advertisement and track their actions through the site. A simpler option: in the student data intake form or survey, include an item asking if they were referred to your school by TV advertising. Want more insight? Ask prospective students how much of a role TV advertising played in sparking them to reach out. We know, it sounds so obvious. But it's amazing how many schools don't do this for TV—or any other tactic.

Consider allocating TV dollars to online and mobile video

If TV doesn't appear to deliver an acceptable return on investment, think about other ways you can use video to build awareness, deliver your message, and drive leads. Work with your agency or internal marketing team to identify online outlets serving your core demographics. There are a number of benefits, starting with the price of entry for online video versus media spends for traditional broadcast TV. Online venues allow you to more easily customize, segment and traffic your video content according to audiences, increasing the likelihood that your message will matter. Finally, online video platforms will provide great flexibility in execution, not only in the length of your video, but in its use. From pre-roll and animated banners to branded content and interactive video, you've got options. Explore them.

Getting in Line at the Advertising Buffet

PRIOR to the Facebook IPO, even a casual news consumer would have thought that Facebook going public was an event somewhere between the Second Coming and National All Debts Are Forgiven Plus Free Ice Cream For Everyone Day. To us, it felt like "Party Like It's 1999 Day" all over again: dot-com stocks are back, baby!

Unfortunately for those who jumped on the bandwagon, F-Day didn't quite live up to the hype. The stock lost more than 60% of its initial value within four months of its IPO. It's anyone's guess whether it can gain the confidence of investors long term.

The financial ups and downs of the platforms we advertise on are important, of course, but Facebook's freefall goes far deeper than just a bunch of investors getting jittery over the numbers. If you want the real reason why Facebook may not be the gilded gravy train it was made out to be, start by looking at its main product: advertising. And as it turns out, its main product is, in the words[110] of Mike Shields of Adweek, "abysmal."

According to Shields, after examining 11,000 Facebook campaigns, Webtrends found that the social network's average click-through rate for ads slipped from 0.063% in 2009 to 0.051% in 2010. At the same time, the cost-per-thousand impressions (CPM) rose from $0.17 in 2009 to $0.25 in 2010. A more recent analysis[111] by TBG Digital found that CPMs increased 41% between Q1 2011 and Q1 2012 while click-through rates decreased 8% from Q4 2011 to Q1 2012. During the same time period, the average cost per fan increased a whopping 43%. Not exactly the kind of performance that warms the cold cockles of investors' hearts.

Or advertisers' either. A few days before F-Day, General Motors cast its vote on Facebook's advertising performance by pulling its entire $10 million advertising budget from the platform. And while that's not even 1% of Facebook's ad revenue[112] for 2012, GM's departure from the service had to have made a lot of the money people nervous. If the number two advertiser[113] in the country doesn't have faith, why should anyone else?

So is GM right and Facebook wrong? On the contrary, based on a tweet from Mary Henige, GM's director of social media, GM's pullout from Facebook might be the ultimate indicator about what's wrong with the advertising industry in general.

In his Businessweek article[114] about GM ditching Facebook, Ben Kunz recounted what happened when he tweeted about GM's actions:

"When I riffed on Twitter, 'Wow, GM yanks $10M from FB…' Mary Henige, GM's director of social media, tweeted back: 'We have more than 8mil friends on FB; not leaving them; engagement & content isn't same as advertising.' Fair point, Mary."

Fair point? Henige's point isn't fair. In fact, we think it's wildly inaccurate, especially considering that GM spends[115] about $30 million developing content for Facebook. She's saying that Facebook content is not advertising? It certainly isn't literature designed to elevate the human spirit[116].

But perhaps we shouldn't be too hard on Ms. Henige. Based on her tweet, she merely suffers from the same delusions shared by most of the advertising industry: That things are somehow the same now as they've ever been with the exception of this pesky digital stuff that they now have to deal with. All that content and engagement stuff is a pain in the back that we have to endure: *real* advertising is the cool stuff we get to show on TV and in glossy magazine spreads, right?

So if the idea of advertising is to get people to do something, why aren't engagement and content seen as advertising?

Ahem. According to the all-knowing Wikipedia, advertising is defined as "a form of communication used to encourage or persuade an audience to continue or take some new action." And though one could quibble with the definition (or the source), we're sure that most of us encountering this definition would recognize it as being mostly true.

So if the idea of advertising is to get people to do something, why aren't engagement and content seen as advertising by folks like Ms. Henige of GM? After all, a Fleishman-Hillard/Harris Interactive study[117] on the influence of digital media on consumer-buying decisions found that 79% of folks on social networking sites across the world used social networking to learn more about brands they were interested in. The same study found that one in five people used Facebook "to obtain information about a brand or product." Considering that, as of October 2012, Facebook's U.S./Canada user base now tops 186 million (more than 50% of the combined population of the two countries) and reaches over one billion people throughout the rest of the world, the lowly duo of engagement and content seems to have the potential for a pretty significant impact on influencing consumer behavior. Kinda like that "advertising thing."

So why in this age of consumers dividing their attention between multiple screens[118], beaming Internet content into their living rooms via Internet-connected TVs[119], cutting the cord in ever-rising numbers[120], watching nearly 40 billion videos[121] online, spending nearly 25% of their online time with social media sites[122], and increasingly shifting their TV viewing from broadcast to online sources and DVRs[123], does anyone continue to discount digital?

We can think of a few reasons, and not all of them are ones that the Mad Men (and Women) of Madison Avenue want to hear.

Global Facebook Penetration
A Country Comparison

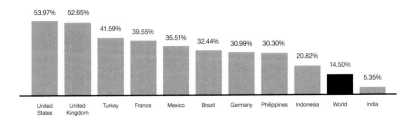

Source: wikipedia.org

Digital isn't ambiguous. It's about performance, pure and simple. Unlike traditional media, there's no wiggle room: Either an online ad delivers or it doesn't. And while some can throw up great clouds of figurative and metaphorical squid ink when confronted with the results of their campaigns, as Ari Jacoby of Online Media Daily puts it[124], "real performance [isn't] subjective. It should be about showing brands how an online marketing effort affects and influences consumer behavior. Anything else is fuzzy logic." In digital, there's nowhere to hide.

There's also the issue of defining what an ad actually is these days. More than 80 years of commercial TV and hundreds of years of print

Digital isn't ambiguous. It's about performance, pure and simple.

advertising have trained us to see advertising as something that comes to us. It interrupts the program that we're watching on TV. It cuts into the music we're listening to on the radio. It gets in the way of us finishing an article. And it pops into our attention sphere while we're out of our homes. It's not something that we seek out. Advertising isn't something we asked for. But it's something we'll accept if it resonates. Legendary adman Howard Luck Gossage once noted[125], "People don't read ads. They read what interests them, and sometimes it is an ad." The observation still holds true, whether consumers admit it or not. The best ads seek us out, grab our attention, and if they're effective, they make damn sure that we remember what they were selling so we can go out and buy it.

Engagement and content on the other hand are a bit more subtle. We have to seek out content and participate in order to engage. Branded content and experiences can't assault us like traditional advertising or hold our attention hostage. It can't scream, "I'm an ad!" But if the experience or the content is good enough, we're happy to install[126] it in our smartphones or pass[127] it along to our friends. We even welcome it when we are on the hunt for something to purchase.

The real issue with advertising today isn't, "Why haven't we figured out how to replicate the attention hostage-taking experience of television advertising online?" but rather, "How are we going to deal with consumers who expect to have total control over their media consumption?" Or, more simply, "How are we going to deal with choice?"

Like it or not, we're smack dab in the middle of the Age of Choice.

Consumers now have a dizzying array of media choices[128] from tablets to phones to video game consoles to PCs to traditional televisions. Nearly half of us watch video online and 37% of us are time-shifting our TV watching. Shipments of Internet-enabled consumer devices are projected to exceed PCs in 2013[129]. Paradoxically, while print consumption is down, new magazine launches are up[130]. Every day the world creates staggering amounts of data…photos, video, audio, and text. We're awash in a sea of choices and can choose to view or read or listen to anything we want, whenever we want, and, increasingly, wherever we want.

Today, the consumer is in control…and she isn't all that interested in giving up that control, especially to advertisers. In the Age of Choice, accomplishing the goal of advertising—encouraging or persuading people to act—means recognizing that, as an advertiser, you're no longer in control. Advertising can only work when we provide content or experiences for engagement that attract rather than interrupt consumers' attention.

Data

EVERYONE'S talking about data these days. For some, it's a discussion of data through the prism of privacy—and the spectrum of opinion is as wide as an aircraft carrier. On one side, consumers are terrified by the amount of information marketers have collected about them. On the other, consumers are apathetic about it: They don't fully grasp how the data may be used, aren't aware of what data's been collected, or simply don't mind as long as it doesn't have a negative impact on them. Most people fall somewhere in the middle.

The data discussion isn't relegated to privacy though. Others are more concerned with the sheer size of it. According to IBM[131], the human race creates 2.5 quintillion bytes of data every day. In fact, 90% of data in the world today was created within the last two years. And while brands collect just a sliver of that total data pie, it's still massive. Everything from credit card numbers to what pair of long underwear you bought for your husband before that cruise to Canada—it's all there. Regrettably, most brands don't have the first clue what to do with it. Far too often they store it and they sit on it, hoping that someone in the company will figure out how to use it.

In many cases, University X may not be collecting data at all. As a result it hasn't the faintest idea about what works, what doesn't, who it's reaching, and who it's not. Any success is usually achieved more by accident than by skill. And any failure is usually a result of not knowing any better.

If University X actually collects data, the situation's nearly as bad. University X isn't sure how to use the information it has to create meaningful messages, to connect with the right students, or to make informed marketing decisions about enrollment, retention, and fundraising. Capturing, analyzing, and acting on data are tasks assigned to the "some day" category of their to-do list.

In this section, we shed some light on the monster that is Big Data and offer some recommendations for how you can tame it—and perhaps even teach it some new tricks.

Data: The Final Frontier

If you believe the hype in the marketing industry press, you'd have to believe that digital marketing departments and agencies are places filled with 20-something hipsters, slinging buzzwords and obsessing over their Klout scores while cranking out flashy websites and viral videos. And for good reason. These places do exist (don't ask us to name names). And if you follow the trade press, you hear about them all the time: 21st century Mad Men so far out on the cutting edge that they're practically in tomorrow. They're cooler than you, smarter than you, and more connected than you'll ever be.

But there's a big difference between hype and results.

Only 10% of digital marketers were capable of running "real-time interactive marketing"— using data to make decisions about messaging and performance at the speed of consumers.

If you've been feeling a little left out of the digital marketing revolution—or just feel like you still have a lot to learn—don't worry: You're in good company. The truth is, a surprising number of higher ed marketers (and agencies) are still trying to figure things out. If going online was the first step in the digital marketing revolution, the next frontier is going to be dealing with the tidal wave of data all those digital activities are generating.

A study from analytics firm PulsePoint, "Bridging the Digital Divide,"[132] looked at "the digital marketing capabilities, top challenges and priorities of nearly 400 senior marketers, agency executives and publishers." PulsePoint's goal was to better understand what is actually going on in the world of marketing these days and discover just how effectively marketers are using digital in their marketing mix.

What they found was pretty scary. While consumers are "moving freely across channels and devices, interacting with brands and content in real-time," the digital marketing industry is, for the most part, seriously lagging behind. The study revealed that only 10% of digital marketers were capable of running "real-time interactive marketing"— using data to make decisions about messaging and performance at the speed of consumers. And while 65% of marketers surveyed claimed that they were able to take a "multi-channel" approach in their digital campaigns (using two or more channels), only 27% of agencies reported that they were capable of actually managing a program in real-time.

When asked why they weren't doing such a good job at real-time interactive marketing and campaign performance measurement, the most common answer was "metrics." While they may be collecting data from all of their campaigns, technical complexities, inability to handle and measure real-time data, and difficulties in assessing return on investment were all sited as reasons they were lagging behind. They just can't keep up with and don't know what to do with the data.

Ad Spending In the U.S.
TV vs. Online

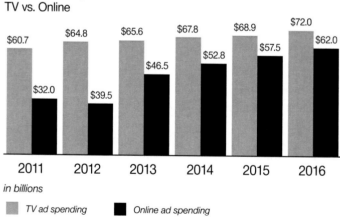

in billions

TV ad spending   Online ad spending

But PulsePoint isn't the only company to hint that marketers and agencies are having a hard time with data. A study conducted by DataXu in 2011 discovered that only about 25% of marketers were able to use data to efficiently allocate their digital marketing spend. With roughly $39 billion spent on online advertising in 2012[133], we can assume that billions of dollars have circled the digital toilet bowl.

Clearly the digital marketing industry is still working on fulfilling the promise of being more accountable than traditional media. Of course, that's not a very high bar to jump: Other than direct marketing, mass-media advertising has rarely been called to task for its accountability. But that's what we had and so we lived with it—even when some studies[134] revealed that as many as 82% of TV ads produced didn't work.

Of course, it's not like anyone's going back to the good old days of what we so quaintly call traditional marketing. Forrester predicts that online marketing spending will come close to $77 billion by 2016. That's nearly double the spending on broadcast TV[135] in 2011 when spending on traditional channels plummeted 161% as digital spending rose 14%[136].

So what's the answer?

It starts with data. Lots of it. For digital marketing to *really* work—particularly in the higher ed arena where success is tied to smart data acquisition, management, and tracking—it has to move beyond flashy gimmicks, viral videos, and hip new social apps. All those things are fine, but they have to be accompanied by smart data collection and analysis of the performance of online marketing programs across multiple channels in real-time. While we've made some strides in this direction, if higher ed digital marketing is going to deliver on its promise, we're all going to have to get down with Big Data.

What's Big Data? The McKinsey Global Institute states[137] that Big Data is "the next frontier for innovation, competition, and productivity." IBM says[138] Big Data is "an opportunity to find insights in new and emerging types of data and content, to make your business more agile, and to answer questions that were previously considered beyond your reach." Forbes simply calls it[139] a "big opportunity."

We call it "knowing how to understand what's going on."

While Big Data has become a buzzword lately, the concept's not that difficult to understand. Whether you're using your debit card to buy lunch, zipping along in your car using your EZPass to skip through tolls, searching Yelp to find a place to eat dinner, or using Google, just about everything we do these days generates data. Lots of it. Remember that stat from earlier? It bears repeating: There are over 2.5 quintillion bytes of data generated worldwide each day, the equivalent of over 130,000 Libraries of Congress.

There are over 2.5 quintillion bytes of data generated worldwide each day, the equivalent of over 130,000 Libraries of Congress.

While people concerned with privacy have become increasingly alarmed by the amount of data the average person generates as they move through their life, the secret is that most of that data just sits around in databases gathering pixel dust. Companies that have figured out how to analyze and make decisions based on that data—Google, Amazon, TRW, and Wal-Mart, for example—have done well for themselves; they've realized the power in understanding how to turn raw data into actionable knowledge. For most businesses, the potential is huge: McKinsey Global Institute estimates[140] that retailers could increase their operating margins by as much as 60% by leveraging the data they're already generating. The U.S. healthcare industry could create $300 billion in value every year by using data to reduce costs and increase efficiencies.

Our industry's no different. The promise of digital marketing has always been based on the data it generates. Knowing what ads are working and which aren't allows advertising to move from creative guesswork to real-time science. Knowing information such as the age, gender, location, and interests of consumers allows advertisers to hyper-target advertising so that the right messages reach the right audiences at the right time. But it's more than that. Being able to serve advertising based on consumer behavior and charge for media based on whether or not an ad generated a response allows publishers to create incredibly attractive and efficient advertising models that need less overhead (the decisions are made by computers) to generate more advertiser satisfaction.

The promise of digital marketing is huge. Fewer wasted ad dollars. Real-time optimization. Up-to-the-microsecond ROI calculation.

Hyper-targeting. Personalized messaging custom tailored to the individual consumer. Advertising Nirvana.

That's the promise. But we're not there yet. In order to fulfill the promise, the industry has to move away from thinking of advertising as some mysterious, sexy secret known only to a few hipper-than-thou acolytes lucky enough to get the culture. The industry has to instead move towards a way of thinking that puts data first. This doesn't mean creativity isn't important—it always will be. In fact, in a future where the ad biz relies on Big Data, creativity will become even *more* important; it will drive messages that cut through the ever-growing digital noise of an always-on, always-connected global marketplace. It'll be increasingly hyper-targeted. Smaller segments, more relevant messaging, and a greater volume of ads needed to reach the population at large. Great creative gets even better when it's coupled with great data. And it gets great results.

Great creative gets even better when it's coupled with great data.

Now, the real question: What does all this mean for marketers in higher education?

Demand more from your agency

Insist that your agency have a detailed strategy for collecting, managing, and making use of the data available to them. Higher education is a competitive and expensive industry to market. Your agency (or internal marketing team) should be driven not only by the message, but by the measurable results that message brings to bear. Work together to develop clear goals and specific data metrics that will eliminate any doubt you may have about the return you're getting on your marketing investment.

Share nicely

While local, state or even national privacy policies may prohibit the sharing of personal data your institution has collected, there is data—both qualitative and quantitative—that you can and should share with your marketing partners. This may seem like a no-brainer, but too often, data sharing falls to the wayside—or worse, it gets forgotten. It's essential to develop a plan for communicating data with partners on a regularly scheduled basis. The data you share—well that's up to you and your marketing partners.

Behavior and preferences for particular student and prospect demographics—the kind of information you might gather from focus groups and surveys—can help your marketing teams refine messages. An ad that has the right message, served at the right time, to the right people will obviously have better results than a shotgun spread of generic messages fed indiscriminately to media outlets. Quantitative data will also offer crucial insight for refining strategy. And it goes beyond the usual suspects like response rates, costs per lead, and page views. Consider any and all data that could provide your partners with a bigger piece of the picture. If you're not sure of what data matters, your agency should be.

The Dirty Little Secret Behind User Data Collection & Tracking

WHILE the previous segment highlighted the importance of sharing data with your marketing partners, we can't ignore the caveats. Privacy's always been a big concern on the Internet. Ever since the invention of "cookies" back in 1994[141], there's been an ongoing and often contentious debate over who gets to collect personal data about users, how that data is collected, and how it's used.

On one side, the marketers, retailers, advertisers, and publishers try to gather as much data as possible in order to target advertising more efficiently, sell more products, and deliver content tailored to users' needs and wants. On the other side, privacy advocates, "hacktivist" groups like Anonymous, and consumer organizations contend that collecting data about online behavior is an invasion of users' right to privacy. While the privacy advocates have won a few skirmishes in the war over the decades, the trend has pointed towards collecting more and more information.

Exhibit A, Google's push to capture and aggregate data from across their many properties (including Google+ and their ubiquitous search engine). Their goal was to create incredibly detailed profiles of users and their online behavior. Many accused Google of betraying their "don't be evil" motto through alleged actions such as bypassing browser privacy settings to track users via cookies[142]. The public took notice, as did government regulators who launched an investigation into Google's actions.

There's no denying that having your behavior tracked online can make anyone a bit uneasy. Even if you're the most straight-laced Web surfer on the planet, the idea that someone, somewhere is looking over your shoulder and recording your every move online is a little too *1984* for many of us. Nobody likes being watched, especially when being watched also includes recording absolutely everything you do.

On the other hand, tracking online behavior has become an integral part of online marketing. While early online ads were usually served up on a straight cost-per-thousand impressions (CPM) basis with little targeting beyond what section in a site they appeared in, ad-serving software has become increasingly sophisticated over the years. Today, behavioral targeting of online ads has become the norm, serving up ads to users based on their search behavior, browsing patterns, and social media interests. While the Holy Grail of online advertising—delivering the exactly right ad exactly at the right time to exactly the right user—hasn't arrived yet, we're a lot closer than we were two decades ago.

But it's not just advertising that's being driven by tracking data; increasingly, publishers are using behavioral data to serve up everything from search results to news articles. In fact, one of the big changes that Google has instituted over the last few years has been to tailor search results based on past searching and browsing behavior. We're not just talking paid search results here; organic search results are being targeted, too.

Facebook also uses behavior to tailor the information we see in our News Feeds, serving up postings from our online friends based on a complex algorithm that takes into account what we post, what we read, and what we "like."

While few Web users are actually paying attention to the terabytes of data being collected on them, the real story is that "Big Brother" (or "Big Advertiser") isn't paying all that much attention either.

While many feel that algorithmic content targeting can be beneficial by serving up more content we want to see and less we don't, others such as *The Filter Bubble*[143] author Eli Pariser have worried that this kind of targeting will lead to a polarization of discourse as users increasingly see only what they want to see and aren't exposed to dissenting viewpoints or information.

And so the Data Wars rage on. While privacy advocates and online marketers continue to fight pitched battles over the ethics and methods of online tracking, it turns out that there's a dirty little secret that nobody's talking about. While few Web users are actually paying attention to the terabytes of data being collected on them, the real story is that "Big Brother" (or "Big Advertiser") *isn't paying all that much attention either.*

A study[144] by Columbia University's Center on Global Brand Leadership and the New York chapter of the American Marketing Association found that more than half of senior-level marketers report that lack of data sharing across their organization is a "major obstacle" to their effectively calculating the ROI of their marketing efforts. Nearly half (45%) of marketers surveyed reported that they're not using data to effectively target their marketing communications and 42% reported that they're not able to link data to individual customers. When it comes to tracking user data from newer platforms (such as social media and mobile channels), even fewer were even collecting information: 35% reported that they collected social media data and only 19% reported that they collected data from mobile users.

One might be tempted to dismiss one survey, but it's harder to ignore when similar results are reported by other studies. In fact, a January 2012 study[145] by business-intelligence firm Empirix found that only 39% of C-level executives in the U.S. and Western Europe reported that their companies were "making the most" out of data generated by prospects and customers. Another survey released in late 2011 by IBM[146] found that more than 70% of global Chief Marketing Officers (CMOs) felt "unprepared" for the explosion of data they're now collecting from customers and prospects.

Nearly half (45%) of marketers surveyed reported that they're not using data to effectively target their marketing communications.

Clearly there's a huge gap between the vision of malevolent omniscience often described by privacy advocates and the reality of companies struggling to stay afloat in the tsunami of data now available to them. While there's no doubt that lots of data is being collected about our online behavior, most companies don't seem to know what to do with it. And even if some in the company want it, it turns out that most aren't equipped to combine multiple streams of data into the kind of coherent total picture that many fear.

Does this mean that advertisers should be striving to eliminate consumers' privacy in an effort to wring out every last drop of behavioral data? No. In fact, our agency believes that too much data can be a dangerous thing for a number of reasons:

There's no "us vs. them" when it comes to tracking consumer behavior

We're all consumers, too. And all that behavioral information gathering also makes us uneasy.

Until the law catches up to the reality of user data collection and storage, it's probably better to err on the side of caution

While one company might have all the best intentions in the world when it comes to collecting, storing, and using tracking data, there has been no definitive legal precedent in regards to protecting that data from being transmitted to other (potentially not-so-ethical) parties who may want to use it. On one hand, decisions handed down in cases such as *Viacom International, Inc. vs. YouTube, Inc.* have said that companies can't be compelled to hand over user data. But other decisions[147] have affirmed that the government *can* get access to your online data without a warrant. Until there's a definitive decision one way or another, there's no way of knowing who can get access to your data nor under what circumstances anyone can be compelled to provide it.

It's one thing to collect data—it's another thing to do something intelligent with it

If you've ever had your Amazon.com recommendations suddenly go haywire after buying gifts for the children in your life (My Little Pony, anyone?) or have been bombarded by ads for products you were searching for long after you've made a purchase, you know the algorithms that govern behavioral targeting aren't exactly perfect. Intelligently using the data marketers collect requires a lot of time and effort. Using it incorrectly can result in irritated customers who go somewhere else.

Paying too much attention to short-term numbers can result in losing sight of your long-term goals

As Ben McAllister points out in his piece in *The Atlantic*[148], companies who become too reactive can fall into what he calls "The Measurement Trap," a focus on short-term thinking that can damage long-term brand value.

Are we saying that measurement is wrong? Absolutely not: Paying attention to advertising channel performance, response rates, user trends, and other campaign key performance indicators (KPIs) is more important now than it ever was. We're long past the days where agencies could just smile and ask their clients to trust that a campaign was working. Accountability is critical. Likewise with targeting: Being able to hyper-target your campaigns to your audiences vastly increases the performance of your advertising (and stretches your marketing dollars, too).

But examining performance trends and targeting customers based on aggregated data is one thing. Collecting personally identifiable information on customers and not being able to protect or intelligently use that data is something else entirely. It's important that we all remain aware of the benefits and drawbacks of capturing user data and work collectively to use it ethically and responsibly.

Student Recruitment

CUTTING through the clutter and staking out a solid position is one thing. But creating a dialogue that leads to participation or enrollment from the right prospects…well, that's a process all its own.

We often hear about the recruitment funnel, the process of guiding prospects toward enrollment while confirming their interest and qualification. What we don't hear discussed as frequently is the time, energy, and money wasted prior to and during this process on efforts that are not working, or worse yet, are driving prospects away.

Let's not be shy here: Student recruitment is usually one of the biggest—if not THE biggest—goal for higher-ed marketers, and it's the one goal they struggle with the most.

University X *really* struggles with it, often lacking the comprehensive strategies that link student enrollment to other parts of its marketing efforts. In doing so, it fails to connect with prospective students effectively and it misses opportunities to successfully manage its efforts using smart monitoring and measurement.

We apologize for only devoting a section of this book to recruitment: This topic deserves a book of its own (we'll get right on that). But for now, let's focus on some of the most pressing issues related to recruitment as part of the larger higher education marketing/communications mix.

Pumping New Life Into Your Prospective Student Leads

WHO doesn't want more leads? Competition for students is tough and getting tougher every day. Today's marketers face intense pressure to increase the leads coming into their organizations. More leads means more prospects. More prospects means more students. Leadership (both administrative and academic) is under intense pressure to boost enrollments in the face of increasing competition, decreasing budgets, and dwindling resources.

All this pressure has led people to do some desperate things. Dickinson State University president Richard J. McCallum decided to create the appearance of higher enrollments by counting as enrollees the members of the general public who'd attended campus events, high-school students seeking dual credit, and businesspeople attending on-campus sessions. All in all, his creative accounting methods added another 180 students to the rolls—a 7% increase[149] in enrollment in a school of 2,500. Not a bad bump!

> **Leadership (both administrative and academic) is under intense pressure to boost enrollments in the face of increasing competition, decreasing budgets, and dwindling resources.**

Unfortunately Bill Goetz, Chancellor of the North Dakota University System, wasn't impressed, especially after several of the "students" contacted for the National Survey of Student Engagement reported back that they'd never been students at Dickinson State. After a very public feud, Chancellor Goetz showed a very unapologetic McCallum the door.

While pressure to boost enrollments has led to college presidents turning to creative accounting measures to show jumps in enrollment, marketers at several colleges were surprised recently when they discovered that someone was using the identity of their schools to bamboozle information out of prospects[150] using a sneaky online bait-and-switch. Marketers discovered that when they searched Google for their schools, mysterious Google ads showed up that they didn't remember buying. When they clicked on the ads, they were often directed to an official-looking landing page that also appeared to be from their institution. They were then prompted to fill out a form for more information about the school. Imagine how shocked they were when an admissions rep from different school called them shortly after they submitted the form.

It's just one of many examples of fraudulent lead generation companies using unethical tactics to generate more leads for their customers (and more money for themselves)—unethical practices that have gotten them into hot water before.

The sad fact of the matter is that schools are using tactics like this because they work—at least sometimes. Just like spammers, they rely on people's ignorance and the ease of reaching huge numbers of people online in the hopes that a few will actually end up taking the bait.

In 2011, many of the online for-profit institutions were called out on aggressive (and fraudulent) marketing tactics. And even though they've spent millions to fight regulation[151], those schools have been forced to comply with how they market themselves. Not surprisingly, they've also seen their enrollments plummet by an average of 14.1%[152] in the first quarter of 2012. Apparently crime did pay.

If you really want to increase your leads in an effort to boost your enrollments, you don't have to resort to virtual Three Card Monte or "Click the bunny to win an iPad" trickery. Be honest about who you are and what your institution offers. Don't be afraid to be clear about your entrance requirements up-front. And don't hide information like tuition and other costs from your prospects. Tell the truth and make it easy for prospects to discover what it's like to go to your institution, whether you have the programs they're looking for, and how much it's going to cost them.

Here are a few more tidbits of advice worth considering:

Focus on generating qualified leads

While it's tempting to be able to report back to the Powers That Be that leads are pouring in as a result of your marketing efforts, those leads won't do you any good if they're not prospects suited to your institution. In fact, there is such a thing as having too many leads. Especially when most of those leads you generate add more strain on your already stretched resources. Even worse, if you're generating leads on a cost per lead basis, those unqualified leads aren't just wasting your time…they're wasting your money, too!

Go where the prospects go

Do your homework about where your targets hang out online and use multiple methods to reach out to them. We employ the "4S's": Search Engine Marketing (paid search), Search Engine Optimization (natural search), Social Media Engagement, and paid Social Media Marketing (ads on social media sites). Working together these cover all the bases, especially when integrated into a larger campaign.

According to an MIT study, a lead contacted within five minutes is 22 times more likely to convert than a lead contacted after 30 minutes.

Convert clicks to leads through great landing pages

What good is it to get someone to click if you can't get their information? Focus on designing a landing page the offers a compelling message with a clear call to action. And fight the urge to fill the page with links to unnecessary content; it only distracts a prospective student from answering your call to action.

Once you get the leads, follow up!

Today, people expect an immediate response. It's not enough to send an automated thank-you page anymore. Work to make sure you build a compelling campaign to move them from interest to application! According to an MIT study[153], a lead contacted within five minutes is 22 times more likely to convert than a lead contacted after 30 minutes.

Monitor your results and be nimble

Lead generation cycles can change unpredictably. One month Facebook is getting all the action. In the next month, it might be Google. Unless you're constantly monitoring your results and optimizing your spend on an ongoing basis, you won't be able to get the leads you want as reliably as you want.

You don't have to be a crook to increase leads, increase yield, and build enrollments. What you have to be is willing to do the work necessary to get the results you want.

Are You Ready for a Closer Relationship with Prospective Students?

UNFORTUNATELY, they might not be ready for you.

With all the buzz about social media as a way of connecting with our audiences, it's tempting to want to jump in whole-hog and start using tools like Facebook to build closer relationships with prospective students, especially if you're going after the demographics that seem to live on social media. While the kids may spend every waking moment Skype-ing and Facebook-ing each other silly, they don't necessarily want to use those kinds of tools to talk to you or your school.

Surprised? We were too when we read in Cappex's "6 Trends in Digital and Mobile Communications for College Admissions in 2011"[154] that Facebook was at the bottom of the list of ways that prospective students wanted to be contacted about schools they were interested in. Even more surprising was that email topped the list (93%) of preferred contact methods followed by snail-mail (65%), cell phone (32%), home phone (26%), and texts (24%). Only 20% of students listed Facebook.

Shocking, huh? After all, isn't everyone desperately trying to figure out their social media strategy in an effort to pursue these heavy-duty social media users? Haven't we all been told, "Email is for old people?" Why don't prospective college students want to use the one communication method they use the most—76% put it at the top of their list according to Noel Levitz's "2010 E-Expectations Report."[155] In fact, social media didn't even make Levitz's "How Do Students Learn about Schools" list. Snail mail (89%), "parents, family, and friends" (80%), and email (79%) were the big winners in that category.

How Students Prefer to Communicate With Schools
A Comparison of Channels

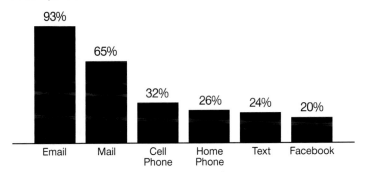

n = 1064 2011 high school graduates
Source: Cappex.com

Why? Why aren't prospective students turning to social media to contact schools and learn more about what they offer? Should we all just scrap our social media recruitment efforts?

No. But we might need to face the facts: We're trying to get too intimate with prospects too fast.

In 1988, social psychologists Reis and Shaver proposed a new and surprisingly simple model for how intimacy develops. Their model, published in the Handbook of Personal Relationships[156], proposes that intimacy has two dimensions: **responsiveness** and **self-disclosure**. Simply put, the more responsive two people are to each other and the more they disclose about themselves in the relationship, the more intimate they become.

If you look at any of the relationships in your life you'll probably find that this model makes a lot of sense. When we first meet someone we're probably not too responsive; phone calls, conversations, meetings—they're probably infrequent at the initial stages. We're also not too likely to disclose too much about ourselves at first either. But as we get to know each other and become closer, the more we're likely to reveal.

Successful relationships build gradually or at a pace that's comfortable to each party. On the other hand, if someone reveals too much too soon or pushes for too much responsiveness it can get downright creepy. Unfortunately, we've all probably been there a time or two.

But while Reis and Shaver's model seems to apply well to one-on-one relationship building, it's also possible to look at it in the context of building relationships with prospects using commercial communications media. And once you map this model against the characteristics of the various methods we use to communicate with customers and prospects, the problem with trying to force initial contact via social media becomes clear: It's just creepy. Too much, too fast.

The chart below illustrates how various media relate to building intimacy according to Reis and Shaver's model.

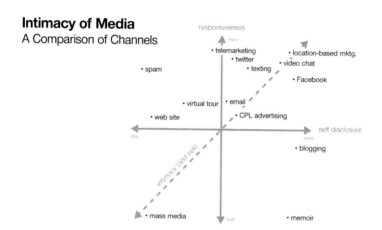

Intimacy of Media
A Comparison of Channels

responsiveness

• telemarketing
• twitter
• spam
• texting
• location-based mktg.
• video chat
• Facebook

• virtual tour
• email
• web site
• CPL advertising

self disclosure

• blogging

intimacy (and risk)

• mass media
• memoir

(based on Reis & Shaver's interpersonal process model of intimacy, 1988)

At one end of the intimacy continuum we've got mass media. It requires little expectation of responsiveness and virtually no self-disclosure. After all, watching a traditional TV spot doesn't require you to give up any information about yourself, and we don't expect a lot of responsiveness. It's an un-intimate, impersonal way of reaching out to prospects.

On the other hand, social media comes with the expectations of both high responsiveness and high levels of self-disclosure. That's kind of the point, isn't it? And even if Facebook has moved to a "like model" that requires less self-disclosure than previously needed, the expectation of Facebook is that connecting with another entity means potentially exposing more of our information than we're comfortable with on a first date.

If you take a close look at the continuum of intimacy as it develops and how various media map to that continuum, the whole process starts to make a lot more sense. Websites, for example, are great for first contact: They're somewhat responsive but require little self-disclosure (unless forced, which is why people don't like to register when they're initially searching for information). Once contact is first made, email becomes a good channel for the next step, slightly ratcheting up both the responsiveness and the self-disclosure requirements. As prospects get to know you better, they're willing to become more intimate in their relationship, allowing greater contact through methods such as texting, phone calls, and (maybe, eventually) social media.

Social media comes with the expectations of both high responsiveness and high levels of self-desclosure.

If you want to build good relationships with your customers and prospects, you have to gradually build trust and intimacy and avoid being creepy by asking for too much information and too frequent contact too soon. Like any good suitor you have to move slowly and be attentive to the cues you're given.

Ask for too much too soon and you might just get dumped.

Recruiting International Students in the Digital Age

THERE'S no doubt that international student enrollments are on the rise. Between the 2006/07 and 2010/11 school years, international student enrollments at U.S. campuses rose nearly 25% according to the National Center for Education Statistics[157]. And whether this rise is a result of globalization or an artifact of the decline of the dollar making a U.S. education more affordable for international students, the fact is that attracting international students is more important than ever— especially for cash-strapped U.S. institutions.

But with budgets shrinking and competition increasing, how do you reach out to the entire world? It turns out that it might be easier than you think.

The most popular reason for engaging in social media was to reach students already engaged in social media activities.

In 2011, Global Campus[158] released an informal survey about the use of social media in international recruiting based on the responses of 30 institutions. While its authors describe the survey as exploratory, it's worth a look for what it reveals about how social media is being used to recruit international students.

Considering some of the core characteristics of social media—open dialogue, instant communication, and low cost access to enormous pools of international prospects—the results of the survey were surprisingly... unsurprising. For instance, rather than turning to social media in order to drive traffic or extend the institution's brand the study found "the most popular reason for engaging in social media was to reach students already engaged in social media activities."

While most respondents did indicate that they view social media as a "more cost effective recruitment strategy," the results also point to limited investment of time and money among the majority of these institutions: Only eight schools reported spending over twelve hours per week on social media activities. Although the respondents seem to recognize the value and potential of social media in their international recruitment efforts, the level of engagement and investment in social media by most of the responding institutions was minimal and the strategies they typically employed were unfocused and passive.

The results beg the question: Why aren't institutions taking advantage of this scalable and accessible resource in their international recruiting efforts? The answer may lie in the responses offered regarding the perceived drawbacks of social media, which included "ambiguous results" and a lack of "clear guidelines or information on effective strategies."

Perhaps the problem isn't a lack of recognition that social media is a powerful tool but rather an overestimation of its power. Besides adhering to the continuum of intimacy—the notion that you have to ease into a relationship with prospect through gradual disclosure and responsiveness—marketers must realize that using social media requires a well thought-out strategy, cultural sensitivity, and a concerted effort to focus its targeting. Optimal use of social media to reach international students requires adhering to the following imperatives:

Maintain a Cultural/Behavioral Approach

As with all behavior, online behavior is overwhelmingly influenced by cultural frames of reference. International outreach can't take a "one-size-fits-all" approach, especially in the world of social media. If you're going to reach out to international students, invest time in researching and analyzing your targets' online behavior and customs in the context of the local culture. Take a global brand like McDonald's, for example. It has thrived because of its ability to create meaningful messages—and relevant products—that appeal to audiences. While they don't lose site of their overall brand identity, they cater their offerings to meet the needs—such as Vegemite on an English muffin in Australia or spinach and parmesan McNuggets in Italy.

Employ Social Media as a Discovery Tool

One of the best ways to learn about prospects is through informal surveys and conversations with the people you want to reach. Strategies that utilize social media properties should be preceded by research into customs, culture, online behaviors, and cultural mores. Try using student assistants (especially those who are members of your target populations) to engage with your prospects online in a social media context.

Leverage Communication and Lead Experience for Qualification

Social media engagement is not only beneficial in terms of reaching wider audiences; it also provides a means of filtering unqualified prospects, particularly in international recruiting. Once you have established a culturally appropriate mode of interaction, two-way communication with prospects provides valuable insights that range from English proficiency to individual interests and aspirations. Using tools such as standardized country-specific Q&A matrices can help streamline this process.

Use a Multi-Pronged Approach to Build Your Brand

Social media engagement is only one part of online recruitment, but it can be a powerful component of a more comprehensive awareness strategy. It can help to establish your institution's reputation in a given region. Today's international students have more choices than ever, and the most qualified students will only make the investment of time, money, emotion and cultural adjustment if they feel that their efforts will pay off. Publishing or linking to faculty research, alumni success stories, and specialized professional opportunities will help international prospects see the value in attending your institution over another.

Track and Monitor

Whether you are using country-specific sites (such as Mixi, Renren, Okrut or Tigtag) or sites like Facebook with a broader global reach, it's important to segment your properties based on the country or region you're targeting. You need a system to track what's working where. Also, monitor the conversation within that area to help manage your reputation. While this can seem like a large undertaking, employing software agents, student assistants, or outsourced resources can help ensure that a cultural misstep or language error doesn't spiral into a crisis among the prospects you're trying to reach.

Big Ideas

WHEN it comes to developments in online marketing, there's a lot of noise out there and even more hype . Whether that hype is of the "utopia's just over the horizon" variety or "the end is near, stock the shelter" pessimism, there's no end to the hyperbole and breathless pronouncements, especially because they generate attention and page-views. The middle ground often gets washed out to sea by the tsunami of overwrought prose generated by the earth-shaking agrandizement of online pundits and self-proclaimed "experts."

In a humble effort to stem the hype-tide, our last section is a collection of reflections on trends we've noticed, general ideas about communications and design, and some other useful morsels we feel will provide you with the weapons you need to beat back the creeping threat of becoming a University X. You may find that some buck conventional wisdom in a curmudgeonly manner or that others may barbeque a sacred cow or two, but we only do so because we've noticed that our clients are best served when we draw their attention to the fact that the Emperor may indeed not be wearing any clothes.

Brainstorming or BS

BRAINSTORMING sessions, free association exercises, judgment-free idea incubators—don't these sound like situations for effective collaboration and bold creative solutions?

Maybe not.

The concept of brainstorming—vigorous group participation in a non-judgmental environment—has long been the darling for those looking to unleash creativity and discover new ways to solve problems. This collaborative spirit has been a driving force in education for decades. But as with so many rituals, the story may be more convincing than the data.

In 2012, journalist Jonah Lehrer wrote a piece for *The New Yorker*[59] that takes some of the wind out of brainstorming. In it, he points to numerous studies that empirically demonstrate that brainstorming usually fails to increase creativity. In fact, it often inhibits it.

Studies have shown that brainstorming usually fails to increase creativity. In fact, it often inhibits it.

So does this mean we all need to lock the doors to our offices or start working from home? Not at all. Collaboration remains the best way to achieve real results. But we need to develop more mature guidelines for the way schools' marketing and communication departments approach it:

Beware the extrovert bias

Many of the best thinkers in history have been introverts. Deferring to the most outspoken and animated participants is extremely limiting and shortsighted. Don't miss out on silent brilliance by misunderstanding the different styles of your collaborators.

Challenge assumptions

It's nice (in kindergarten) to be in a judgment free environment. But if debate is silenced, differing perspectives and critical thinking are stifled. You owe it to the process to tease out the most relevant thinking rather than appeasing everyone.

Build consensus around hard data

Beginning with the irrefutable is the best way to avoid conflict. Competing egos and opinions are best mitigated by the facts.

Utilize relationships, don't ignore them

Personal dynamics don't magically disappear when your team sits down together to tackle a challenge. Take advantage of the relationships that exist to build on the already present honest respect.

Foster genuine, not enforced, respect

All of us are judgmental and ego-driven to some degree. Trying to pretend we aren't is counter-productive. Judgment will be there whether it's open or not. But it can only be helpful when it's respectfully voiced and tested by debate. In the adult world where we are (hopefully) working, respect is earned—or unearned—by how we communicate.

The Ghosts of Higher Education Past, Present, and Future

OUT of all the industries based on the production and distribution of information (and make no mistake about it…music, books, TV shows, and films are just information), there's one industry that, for the most part, is still partying like it's 1955: higher education.

Taking the online universities out of the equation for a second, traditional colleges share most of the characteristics of the "old media" industries:

They're rigid about how they want to deliver their product

Teachers deliver content to a group of students and only do so in classrooms (whether physical classrooms or online courses).

There's a very high barrier to entry

College is increasingly expensive—and increasingly under scrutiny for the high levels of debt students are graduating with. And starting a college is incredibly difficult, not only from a financial standpoint (we're talking tens if not hundreds of millions of dollars to build an actual college campus) but also from the standpoint of government regulation and industry accreditation.

They're resistant to changes in consumer demand and behavior

In a world where kids spend as much time communicating electronically as they do face to face, where most of us expect to change careers (or, at least employers) several times during our lifetimes, and where we're exposed to as much information in a day as an 18th century scholar may have been exposed to in his lifetime[160], colleges are pretty much the same places they've been for hundreds of years. A time-traveling university student from the 1800's would probably feel at home in the lecture hall of today (as long as they got over the presence of laptops and jeggings). While a demand exists for faster, more flexible delivery, most traditional schools stick to the same models they've used to deliver their product for literally hundreds of years.

They're still bound by physical space and time

Colleges still deliver their consumer product (teaching) in a particular place at a particular time. Like the broadcast networks of the past, if you want something in particular, you'd better be prepared to show at a certain time or expect to miss it. Yes, many offer online options, but those online courses typically run within a specific period of time. Miss it and you've missed out.

Differentiation is getting more and more difficult in an increasingly connected world

Next time you read a physical newspaper or magazine that contains a number of ads for different colleges (ads for MBA programs are especially good for this exercise), try a little experiment: take your thumb and cover up the logo on one of the ads and try to guess which school the ad is pitching. Chances are you're going to have a hard time guessing the name of the school. In the past, location was a differentiator. Today, as more and more schools go online, those who can't make a case for why they're better than their competition (other than their convenient location) are going to have an increasingly difficult time competing in a crowded marketplace.

They're rigidly hierarchical

There are professors and there are students; students are expected to dutifully learn what the professors teach them. While the rest of the world has been transformed by the principles of the open source movement, online collaboration, and virtual organizations, the "sage on the stage" is still the prevailing model in many schools. The idea that professors and students might actually be able to collaborate or that students might be able to learn by collaborating with each other with little or no guidance from an "expert" is unheard of.

They're having their lunch handed to them by their competitors who have responded to the changes brought about by digital communications

The University of Phoenix has over 380,000 students[161]. Arizona State (the largest public university) had a little over 58,000 students[162] in 2010. Even if you count entire university systems[163], Phoenix's 380,000 students would put it in fourth behind The University System of Ohio (478,000), The State University Of New York (SUNY) system (467,845), and The California State University system (417,000). Not bad for a school founded in 1976.

More than half the adults in the U.S. have had some college education.

The plight of higher ed has tentacles that reach beyond the industry's boundaries. Marketers in all verticals should pay attention. Here are a few reasons:

It's a huge industry

By most estimates, higher education is more than a $260 billion industry[164].

It touches all of us

More than half the adults in the U.S. have had some college education[165] and chances are if you're a successful marketer, you've been to college.

It will impact our future

According to Google's Eric Schmidt[166], today we produce as much information in two days as all of human civilization did up to 2003. The only way to keep up is to keep learning. Add to that the increasing need for higher and higher credentials to get jobs[167], and chances are all of us have a lifetime of learning in front of us.

It affects every level of our society

From jobs to innovation to politics, there are few aspects of our lives that aren't changed by what's going on in education.

It's a case study of how the Internet disrupts an industry

If you missed the crazy early days when the music industry was turned on its ear by disruptors such as Napster and iTunes, don't fret: Just keep an eye on what's going to happen to higher education over the next decade to better understand the real impact of the digital revolution.

As gloomy as all this might sound, don't get us wrong: We're optimists when it comes to the future of education. There's a lot of innovation going on out there in terms of new models, including the free online universities such as Khan Academy[168] and University of the People[169], Apple's iTunes U[170], and Sophia[171], a fascinating startup dedicated to creating a social space for teaching, learning, and education.

Yes, there have been problems with for-profit institutions (many of them online) that took advantage of the turmoil in the industry[172], but they're starting to be reined in. And innovation is starting to move to the forefront with initiatives such as MIT's OpenCourseWare[173] and other schools offering free online courses[174] and alternative means of delivery.

But there's a long way to go and a lot to change. Issues with quality, standards, assessment, sustainable business models, access, pedagogy, and online education platforms are just a few that will have to be addressed if higher education is going to reinvent itself like so many of the other information industries. While we'll have to wait to see the new face of education, one thing's for sure: It *will* change. And those changes will impact all of us.

Higher Ed 3.0

THERE'S been plenty of talk in recent years about the future of higher education as tuition costs soar, student loan debt inches towards the $1 trillion mark, public confidence in college as a path to success dims, and government support for higher education continues to erode. But while all these factors—along with increasing competition, globalization, and the decline in the U.S. economy—certainly are having a large impact on the institution of higher learning, the *real* changes coming down the pike might be a lot more disruptive. And they'll be driven more by what's going on online rather than what's going on in Washington or on Wall Street.

Online enrollments have shown growth greater than 10% year-over-year.

There's nothing new about the notion of Higher Ed 2.0: the push for schools to provide online courses. Colleges and universities have been using the Internet for remote teaching since the mid 1990's[175]. According to the most recent available numbers published by Sloan[176], over 6 million students were taking at least one online course in 2010. That's over half a million more than were enrolled in online classes during the previous year. While overall student enrollments have increased by barely 1%, online enrollments have shown growth greater than 10% year-over-year. At this point, according to the Sloan study, nearly one third of all college and university students have taken at least one online course. More surprising: two out of three students ranked the quality of the online learning experience as being either the same or better than what they received face-to-face.

How Does the Online Learning Experience Compare to In-Person Learning?
Based on Student Survey

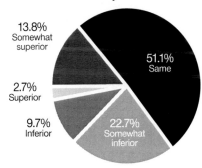

13.8%
Somewhat
superior

2.7%
Superior

9.7%
Inferior

51.1%
Same

22.7%
Somewhat
inferior

Source: Cappex.com

The important thing to remember about these figures is that "online education" isn't only referring to the seemingly ubiquitous private for-profit institutions that many folks associate with online. The growth in the sector is across the board and, in fact, the Sloan report finds that it's the private, for-profit institutions that are showing the slowest growth; most are reporting either flat or declining enrollments. The growth, it appears, is happening in what many consider the traditional higher education sector: public and private not-for-profit colleges and universities. Far from resisting online education, 65.5% of Chief Academic Officers reported to Sloan that "online education is critical to their institution's long-term strategy."

Higher Ed 2.0 is entering a new phase. At the same time that traditional colleges and universities are moving their paying students online, some of the biggest names in higher education are beginning to offer free versions of their courses to anyone who wants to sign up. Massively Open Online Courses[177] (otherwise known as MOOCs) got off to a modest start in 2008 when the University of Manitoba offered an online course that attracted 2,300 students. But it really took off in the Fall of 2011 when Sebastian Thrun of Stanford and Peter Norvig of Brown offered an artificial intelligence course to the world that attracted

160,000 registrants.

Harvard, MIT, and UC Berkeley launched edX.org[178] in 2012 to offer open courses to anyone who wanted to take them. Daphne Koller and Andrew Ng of Stanford launched Coursera[179] in 2012. Serving over one million registered users, the platform currently offers courses from 16 different universities on topics ranging from business to medicine.

Welcome to Higher Ed 3.0, folks.

While the popularity of MOOCs and the growing enrollments in online courses are interesting as indicators of the market's desire for quality, flexibility, and access, they have even greater importance as harbingers of what higher education's going to look like in the future. They offer glimpses of how the Internet is about to disrupt higher education in the way that so many other industries have been disrupted over the past decade and a half.

In order to understand why, take a quick step backwards in time and look at how education has worked for centuries. While variations have cropped up here and there, the model has essentially been the same: A scholar develops knowledge through training and research and then imparts that knowledge to his or her students. While some larger and more affluent universities can afford to provide assistance to the professor in the form of graduate assistants, the process of education is, for the most part, crafted and delivered by one person to those who can fit into his or her classroom.

In many ways this model isn't all that different than the pre-industrial revolution craftsman. In the days before the industrial revolution, products were produced by an expert craftsman who probably learned his trade through a long process of apprenticeship and by working to perfect his technique. The craftsman handcrafted products one at a time and sold them to a limited local or regional market. Often the craftsman had little local competition because geography and population limited the size of the market he had to sell to. A village could only support so many blacksmiths or cabinetmakers.

The industrial revolution changed all this. First, industrialization allowed for the mass production of goods by using machinery to increase the speed of production and assembly-line procedures to allow people with simple training to contribute to the factory's production by performing one simple, repetitive task. Advances in mechanization, such as the steam engine, also allowed producers to distribute their products to a much wider audience across a much larger geographical area. The mass production of common household products pushed out the local craftsperson; a factory could make them cheaper and faster than he ever could. The result was consolidation of the means of production into the hands of the few who could put up the capital to build the factories (to make the products) and the railroads (to distribute them). The revolutionary part of the Industrial Revolution was about controlling the means of mass production and controlling the means of mass distribution.

Until recently, the model of higher education was fairly pre-industrial. The university served as the village where faculty (craftsmen) worked after having toiled away as apprentices in graduate school; eventually they'd leave their home villages (university) to ply their trade somewhere else. What they produced was knowledge, and this knowledge was distributed to their students (customers), up close and personal in classrooms. In this model, production is limited because knowledge is handcrafted by highly trained individuals and distribution is limited because teaching can only be done face-to-face.

Enter the Internet. What the Internet provides is a new means of distribution that allows knowledge to be propagated on a global scale for little or no cost. The producer (the professor) no longer has to have his or her market for their teaching limited to face-to-face distribution. Now, it's simply a matter of putting it up on the web in an online course or a MOOC and distributing it to the whole world. All of a sudden location ceases to matter and the power of the producer of knowledge to produce and sell to an audience becomes virtually unlimited.

As we've seen over the past decade with other industries based on intellectual property—primarily music, film, and book publishing—when the product (the sounds, the images, and the words) is separated from the medium it was previously delivered on (records, DVDs, and physical books), business models built on control and distribution of information in physical form can no longer survive. The record and film industries misunderstood this and are slowly dying. They *thought* they were selling records and DVDs when what they were really selling was the *information* contained on that media. When the digital technology allowed the information to be separated from the medium and the Internet provided a worldwide distribution mechanism for that information, these businesses were doomed. They may be still limping along, but ask yourself: When's the last time you visited a record shop or a video store? One visit to iTunes (or Netflix or Hulu) is all you need.

> **For centuries, the model of higher education has been based on the same principles of controlling the means of production and distribution of information to a limited geographic area. Move that model to the Internet, and it doesn't work anymore.**

For centuries, the model of higher education has been based on the same principles of controlling the means of production and distribution of information to a limited geographic area. Move that model to the Internet, and it doesn't work anymore. On the Internet, one university is just as close to its students as any other; typing in one URL is just as easy as typing in another. Once a college or university goes online, it is no longer competing based on the attractiveness of its physical location, the opulence of its student amenities, or how easy it is for part-time students to reach after work.

While a university may have been able to charge a premium when its key competition was on the other side of the country (therefore limiting its pool of prospective undergraduates), it simply doesn't work that way anymore. In the online world, a student can go to Google (or a specialized search engine for online courses such as Noodle[180]) and find the course or the school that fits them perfectly for a price they can afford.

Of course, we're still a ways away from the scenario portrayed here. Today most students still take face-to-face classes and geography plays a big factor in the decision about a student chooses to go. MOOCs may offer free courses from top-tier universities, but MOOCs (for the most part) don't offer credit or any other recognized credential for students who enroll for the free version. Faculty, even if they're teaching online, are still the primary creators and distributors of the information they teach—as long as they're expected to interact with their students, answer questions, and participate in discussions. The village may have expanded its borders a bit, but most of the goods it produces are still being distributed to a limited range of customers.

For now. There are already attempts to bridge the chasm between free or discounted courses and earned degrees. For example, in the fall of 2013, the University of Wisconsin, will give people the option to earn their bachelor's degrees in select majors simply by successfully completing competency tests[181]. At the very least, it'll be an interesting experiment. Or it just may shatter the model of higher education as we know it.

As Stewart Brand so famously said, "Information wants to be free."[182] And while his comment has often been misinterpreted to mean, "Information doesn't want to be paid for," what he really meant is that the nature of information is that it is difficult (if not impossible) to bind it to a particular place or medium. This may have been difficult to comprehend in the world of 1984 when he first made this statement; most information at the time was contained on analog media. But it's not hard to understand at all in a world where information is digital and can be copied and transmitted at the speed of light. If we're to begin to imagine the future of higher education, we need to remember this.

While your role as a marketer may limit your ability to respond to this looming threat from an infrastructural or pedagogical level, you can certainly be the bell-ringer. Make decision makers in your school aware of these trends. Help them grasp the benefits of addressing (and even embracing) them. More importantly, give them an idea of the consequences of ignoring the shift.

How Content Curation May Save (College) Marketing

"CURATION" is a buzzword, even if it isn't technically a word... unless you count the 14th century French definition meaning "to cure". Launching[183] into the blogosphere virtually from nowhere in 2009, it's now one of those terms that's essential to any digital marketer on the cutting edge—or for anyone who wants to sound like one.

Curation has now come to mean the act of sorting through the vast amounts of content on the web and presenting it in a coherent way, organized around specific topics. Unlike automated services (such as Google News), the essential difference of curation is that there's a human being doing the sifting, sorting, arranging, and publishing. Just as a museum curator must decide which artifacts to display during an exhibition, an online curator decides what information available online is appropriate and relevant to her audience.

Just as a museum curator must decide which artifacts to display during an exhibition, an online curator decides what information available online is appropriate and relevant to her audience.

If you're a web veteran, you're probably wondering how this is any different than what people have been doing online for years. After all, even the earliest home pages usually included lists of favorite links, sometimes curated daily. The portal craze of the 90's was basically the same thing blown up to epic proportions, with billions (yes, billions) invested in portal sites that aggregated content from across the web.

Remember: Content is king! And while blogs started out as personal web logs, they didn't find success until they moved away from musings about cat behavior and toward serving up nifty links to a hungry audience. Check out the 15 most highly trafficked blogs today and every one of them is primarily about directing us to other stuff.

So what's the big deal about curation? The cynic in us wants to say that it's just about reinvigorating the concept of bloggers as editors of the web. And that is a big part of it. But there's one thing that we have now that we didn't have in the 90's…the mass adoption of social media. And that's where the difference comes in.

NYU Professor Clay Shirky provides one of the best explanations[184] of the role of curation in today's web: "Curation comes up when search stops working…[and] when people realize that it isn't just about information seeking, it's also about synchronizing a community."

It's the community part that's at the heart of the whole curation movement. It's also the most powerful element when it comes to curating content as a way of drawing traffic and attention in your marketing efforts. Just as a carefully curated museum exhibit is sure to draw like-minded people together, carefully curated content on the web has the potential to attract and build an online community of people who are into the same stuff.

Making curation work for your school is a lot easier said than done. As countless would-be content curation kings (and queens) have found out, just gathering a lot of links together doesn't guarantee anything except that you'll spend a lot of time curating links. You need to commit resources to both curation and promotion if you're going to be successful. And that's just the first step. To truly succeed as a curator, you need to think like a curator (not just an aggregator) and keep the following in mind:

People matter

Your goal should be to build a community, and communities are made up of people. You need to know your audience intimately and have an innate sense for what they're interested in. And like any good social media effort, you also need to nurture that community through your actions. In some instances you may have multiple communities, each serving a particular audience such as students, the business community, donors, or alumni.

It's a commitment

Just like any social media effort, unless you clearly state from the beginning that you're doing this for a limited time for a specific reason (such as curating content around a student film festival), the expectation is that you're going to be an ongoing resource for your readers. Bailing out unexpectedly is damaging to your brand and your reputation.

What you leave out is as important as what you leave in

Obviously, you can't include everything online in your curation efforts. And you don't want to. The content you include (and exclude) speaks to your university's point of view about a particular topic. Think of it as writing with links. For example, how much of your content will promote what's happening on campus? What about what's happening with alumni? Or crucial application deadlines? Or what's happening in an industry your students will be searching for jobs in? Choose your content carefully and make sure it's consistent with your overall messaging, brand strategy, and audience.

Exhibitions vs. permanent collections

How often you refresh your content is your choice. There will always be a continuous fire hose of content spewing out on the web. But you might want to think about the "classics" that should stay in your collection (such as weekly student events) and what should be rotated out (like an event featuring a particular speaker). You may even want to collect content around a particular sub-topic and archive it if it's worthy of being saved.

Think "niche."

There are plenty of sites out there now that cover broad topic areas and have large, embedded audiences. Drawing readers away to a collection that covers a similar broad topic can be tough…if not impossible. If you want to curate a collection and draw attention, you'll probably have better luck focusing on a niche topic specific to your university's strengths, geography, history, or values. Heck, if our little city of Baltimore can support a Visionary Art Museum, the Great Blacks in Wax museum, a Tattoo Museum, and The National Museum of Dentistry, then your school can certainly find its own corner of the content universe to exist within.

Design matters

Yup. We said it before, and we'll say it again. As usability guru Don Norman stated so well, "Attractive things work better." Throwing up a collection to try to cash in on the curation bandwagon isn't enough. You need to focus on designing a user experience that's not only attractive but usable. Ideally the design should contribute to the overall experience, highlighting the most important content, guiding users to what they're looking for, and fostering community.

Seven Radical Disruptions to Business Every College Marketer Should Know About

If you look at industries disrupted by the Internet over the past 15 years, you'll find that most have been rocked by the following trends:

1. **A shift in power from producer to consumer.**
    How many people use travel agencies now that we have the power to book our own flights? How many of us go to a car dealership without researching purchases online first?

2. **Increased competition brought about by radically reduced barriers to entry.**
    When you don't have to build, buy, or lease physical infrastructure anymore, it's a lot cheaper to start a business than it used to be.

    Regardless of how carefully a brand crafts its messaging now, anything can happen once people start talking about it online.

3. **Heightened expectations for service and responsiveness now that customers are used to anytime, anywhere connectivity.**
    While many companies haven't gotten a great handle on this, we've definitely reached the point where very few people send complaint letters through the U.S. Postal Service when they have a problem.

4. **Loss of control of brand messaging brought about by social media (and, to be fair, increased access to global markets and global brand recognition).**

   Regardless of how carefully a brand crafts its messaging now, anything can happen once people start talking about it online.

5. **Traditional business models have been radically disrupted due to an inability to control product distribution.**

   The record industry's biggest mistake? They thought they were selling discs. They weren't. They were selling information on those discs. And once that information can be digitized and sent anywhere in the world instantaneously, the old models don't work anymore.

6. **Pressure from consumers to be able to buy and use their products anytime and anywhere.**

   While the entertainment industry still wants to fight this trend, the fact remains that most people aren't too happy when they're told that they can't use their purchase on multiple devices. Kudos for the Kindle app (available on just about every platform) for leading the way here.

7. **Elimination of physical location as a differentiator or asset.**

   When people have to physically go to your store to buy what you're selling (or if you have to ship physical goods to stores so that people can buy them) location matters. If what you're selling is information, who cares where you are?

If you look at nearly any industry based on information—travel, entertainment, publishing, journalism—they've been irrevocably transformed over the past 10 to 15 years because of these trends. Oh, they might still be thinking they can legislate, regulate, or use technology to mitigate the effects of these changes. But the rest of us know (at least those of us who don't work in those industries), that they're fighting a losing battle. No matter how much industries (cable providers and mobile carriers are the best examples) that are based on moving data around want to fight it, the fact is that the trend vector points one way. They're destined to be conduits for data.

No matter how much the music, film, and television industries throw digital rights management technologies at the problem, no matter how many obnoxious licensing deals they cut, and no matter how many people they sue, these information industries inevitably will be forced to admit that things can never go back to they way they used to be. And publishers—well, it's pretty obvious at this point that if they don't embrace e-books, they're sunk. Just ask the folks in the newspaper biz.

To be fair, all of these industries have been making adjustments over the years. Still many continue to kick and scream as they are dragged into the digital future.

If they don't give customers want they want, when they want it, and how they want it, someone else will. Can you say "Blockbuster?"

The Not-So-Distant Future of Distance Learning

Over the past few years, open source systems such as Moodle and Sakai have been making inroads into the online classroom space, slowly edging out proprietary systems such as Blackboard.

PEARSON and Google are poised to disrupt the entire learning management system (LMS) industry. They're partnering to release a free and open platform that combines online course management, social networking, GoogleDocs integration, e-books (and other learning materials) supplied by some of the biggest textbook publishers, and an entirely new paradigm for course portability[185]. And while this new partnership will be sure to turn the world of online learning on its ear (and seriously threaten Blackboard's[186] already tenuous position as the LMS leader), the implications of the new venture go far beyond just a new, free way for colleges to offer online courses.

Google/Pearson's OpenClass system[187] isn't the first free online learning tool. Over the past few years, open source systems such as Moodle[188] and Sakai[189] have been making inroads into the online classroom space, slowly edging out proprietary systems such as Blackboard. At the same time, startups such as Odijoo[190] and myicourse[191] have cropped up as DIY alternatives targeted towards audiences such as corporate HR departments, religious organizations, training companies, or freelance wannabe teachers who want to share their knowledge with the world (and maybe make a few bucks at the same time). Online, for-profit universities such as the University of Phoenix or Laureate Education's various online offerings have experienced great financial success leveraging the concept of lifelong learning as a necessary component to remain competitive in the workplace; now it seems as if entrepreneurs everywhere have been searching for the Next Big Thing when it comes to online education.

But so far, no one platform has risen to the top. Some—especially the "set up your own online class and make money from it" learning platforms—have suffered from the classic chicken-or-the-egg problem so common with online applications or communities: How do you attract both content providers *and* consumers? If potential students aren't aware of what a site like Odijoo offers, they aren't going to come. And if no students come, nobody's going to take the effort to create new courses.

OpenClass, on the other hand, looks like it has the potential to become the biggest game changer in the industry since Blackboard took hold back in the late 1990's. First, it's being launched by Pearson and Google—hardly unknown quantities in the online world. Second, it's free and will be hosted on Google's mighty server farms (instead of on university servers); that's a tough combo to beat for cash-strapped, resource-thinned institutions. Thirdly, it's going to be integrated with GoogleDocs, Google's popular, high-quality, collaborative online office software suite already in use by many institutions (as well as by companies and individuals). For today's penny-pinching university CIO looking to replace aging homebrewed systems, ditch hefty yearly licensing fees, or simply gain the peace of mind (and job security) that a well-known brand offers, OpenClass seems like a no-brainer.

OpenClass takes a Facebook-like approach to online learning, allowing students to see a news feed of activities in all their classes, regardless of where they're taking them. Not only will this mean a single login for students who might be taking classes from multiple institutions (or taking multiple classes at a single institution), it also means they can take classes at more than one place at a time through a single interface (provided all the institutions they're learning from use OpenClass).

This feature alone has huge implications for the future of non-credit/continuing education. While it might be rare for someone seeking a degree to take classes at different schools, professionals who need to learn new skills (but don't need credit) can now pick and choose from any institution offering courses through OpenClass. In effect, continuing ed students will be able to create their own virtual university consisting of the best offerings from around the web. And much like the way the music industry was radically transformed when consumers began picking and choosing the individual songs they wanted to download (instead of having to purchase them bundled on CDs), OpenClass has the potential to shake the business of continuing education to its core by creating an open market for learning in a way that hasn't been possible before.

Things get even more interesting when it comes to how OpenClass might impact instructors' lives. Like students, teachers also have a single profile from which to direct all their activities in OpenClass. Instructors who teach at more than one institution (fairly common for professional adjuncts out there who need to teach many classes to make ends meet) will be able to administer all their courses from their single OpenClass profile. Not only does this capability help create a free agent system where teachers become independent from the institutions they teach for, but it also provides a potential platform that can turn teachers into independent agents able to sell high-performing courses to the highest bidder. If this happens it'll be interesting to see how university intellectual property rules and contracts change as it becomes trivial to move curriculum from one school to another. Fights over who owns the courses (the school that paid someone to teach a course or the instructor who developed the course) are sure to follow.

It's not all rosy though. In 2012, OpenClass announced integration with CourseSmart, an online provider of e-books and online learning materials created by a consortium of some of the biggest names in the textbook publishing industry including Pearson, McGraw-Hill, and Wiley. This development is sure to raise some anti-trust issues by allowing seamless integration between OpenClass and the materials provided by top publishers. Unless OpenClass also makes it easy for other publishers to integrate their content, they're going to be in for some major problems—especially at a time when textbook publishers are coming under increased scrutiny for their high-priced products.

Considering the ubiquity of Google and Pearson in the educational industry, OpenClass can't be seen as just another startup in the LMS space. Unlike its predecessors, OpenClass has the potential for revolutionizing how higher education is delivered by providing a common platform that untethers the student and the teacher from the institution. OpenClass might not be just another learning platform: It might just become an open marketplace for learning that radically changes the model of higher education that's existed for hundreds of years.

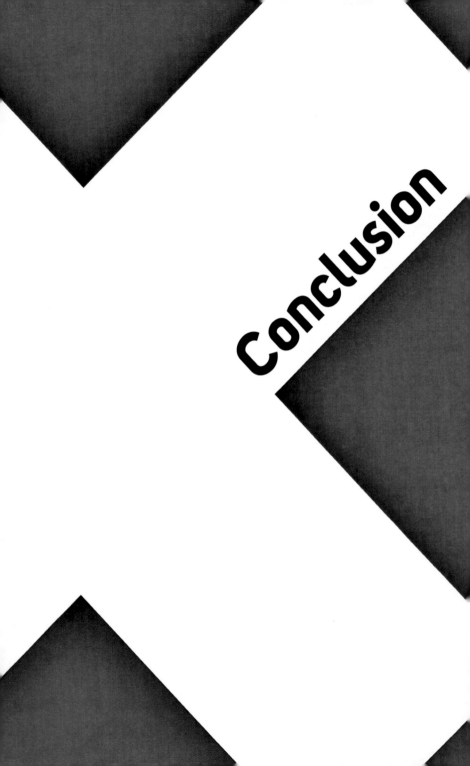

Conclusion

RALPH Waldo Emerson said, "The secret of education lies in respecting the pupil." Like most quotes from smart people, it could apply to a lot of things in life. So allow us to bend it a bit for our own purposes: "The secret of marketing education lies in respecting the times we live in." Not quite as catchy, but still, you get the idea.

There's a seismic shift in higher education and the way our society views it. We can't take anything for granted. For 99.5% of colleges and universities, there isn't an option to simply sit by, polishing the school seal as a line of dump trucks drop piles of applications at the front door of the admissions office. We're in an era of intense competition, not just with other schools, but with growing doubts about whether a college education is even worth the time, trouble, and expense anymore. There's no more room for University X.

So where does this leave us? Well, if we've done our jobs, you're walking away from this book with some useful tidbits that will impact the way you approach your challenges every day. More importantly, we hope you've seen the value in looking beyond the industry of higher ed for smarter approaches to keeping college relevant for a new generation of students.

The only way to survive is to embrace this new landscape and adapt to it. Be open-minded. Be proactive. And above all else, be relevant. Excavate the hidden values in your brand that resonate with today's students. Admit that smart design and ease-of-use aren't just for vacuum cleaners; they're critical to earning respect—and keeping it. Seek to better understand your audiences and speak to them the way they want to be spoken to, where they want to be spoken to, when they want to be spoken to. And, finally, don't get too comfortable. Today's trends in higher ed become yesterday's news before you've had a chance to read tomorrow's headlines.

Have questions about the book? Looking for some advice? Or just have something to add? Don't be shy. Let's keep the conversation going. Drop us a line anytime.

Andres Zapata: Andres.Zapata@idfive.com
                   @iduxwatch

About idfive

IDFIVE is an integrated marketing agency serving higher education, non-profit, and other organizations that make the world a better place. We combine our strategic marketing approach, our expertise in building interactive experiences, and our dedication to lifelong learning to tell amazing stories for the most respected brands. As the minds behind our Informed Design approach, idfive's key partners, Dr. Sean Carton and Andres Zapata, have become leading thinkers in the realm of higher education and not-for-profit marketing.

Dr. Sean Carton

Sean was the founder of one of Baltimore's first Web development firms in 1995, the founding Dean of the School of Design and Media at Philadelphia University, and the co-author of one of the first books about the Web (*The Mosaic Quick Tour* series) in 1993.

Sean has published eight books about the Internet, technology, business, and video games and writes regular columns for ClickZ.com (the leading online advertising industry website) and Publish.com as well as contributing to magazines such as *Wired*, *Revolution*, *Stim*, and *POV*. He has undergraduate degrees in English and Psychology from UMBC, an MA in English Literature from the University of Maryland College Park, and a Doctorate in Communications Design from the University of Baltimore.

Andres Zapata

Andres is a communicator. He ensures progress through connection, understanding, simplicity and clarity. As an adjunct professor at MICA's acclaimed MFA in Graphic Design, he works with the nation's most talented interactive designers. When he is not teaching, he runs idfive. As an accomplished usability and experience designer, Andres is always looking for ways to simplify, enhance and improve interfaces.

Andres' client work has been recognized with numerous awards including numerous Webbies, Addies, CASEs, and IMAs. Other honors include Maryland's Best, smartCEO, and the New York Art Director's Club. He has a B.A. in sociology and communication from Goucher

College, an M.A. in design from the University of Baltimore, and an M.B.A. from the Johns Hopkins University.

Pete Meacham

Throughout his career, Pete has worked with universities, NPO's, and businesses of all sizes, from Baltimore to Beijing, helping them align their communications efforts with the needs of their stakeholders.

In addition to idfive clients, Pete has contributed his expertise in cultural dynamics, media, and market analysis, to organizations such as US-Pacific Rim International, Maryland Public Television, Himmelrich Public Relations, Cynergy Global, Becker Professional Education, and Agora Publishing.

Pete has a BA in English Literature from Goucher College, and an MBA from the University of Baltimore/Towson University joint program.

Matt McDermott

Matt has worked on integrated marketing campaigns for brands and organizations including University of Maryland, University of Baltimore, Johns Hopkins University, National Geographic, the National Security Agency, and the U.S. Navy. Much of his work over the last decade has focused on content strategy, new media, and social marketing–disciplines that thrive on engagement, conversation, and good old-fashioned storytelling.

He holds undergraduate degrees in English and Mass Communications from Towson University and a Master's in Teaching from the Johns Hopkins University.

He also sits on the board of directors for the American Advertising Federation's Baltimore chapter and has contributed to a number of publications including *The Baltimore Sun* and *Advertising Age*.

Citations

1.   Social Demographics: Who's Using Today's Biggest Networks [INFOGRAPHIC].
     (n.d.). Mashable. Retrieved from: http://mashable.com/2012/03/09/social-media-
     demographics/

2.   Getsatisfaction.com. Retrieved from: info.getsatisfaction.com/rs/getsatisfaction/images/
     IncyteGroup_Whitepaper_Q32012.pdf

3.   comScore Releases December 2012 U.S. Online Video Rankings - comScore, Inc. (n.d.).
     Analytics for a Digital World - comScore, Inc.. Retrieved from: http://www.comscore.com/
     Insights/Press_Releases/2013/1/comScore_Releases_December_2012_U.S._Online_Video_
     Rankings

4.   Research Blog: Impact of Organic Ranking on Ad Click Incrementality. (n.d.). Research
     Blog. Retrieved from: http://googleresearch.blogspot.com/2012/03/impact-of-organic-
     ranking-on-ad-click.html

5.   David, E. (n.d.). Research from: Harvard, MIT, Pinpoints Hard Lead Conversion Lessons
     .... Upload & Share PowerPoint presentations and documents. Retrieved from: http://www.
     slideshare.net/B2BLeadRoundtable/research-from:-harvard-mit-pinpoints-hard-lead-
     conversion-lessons-with-easy-solutions

6.   Leads360 Study | Building The Optimal Response Strategy. (n.d.). Leads360 Lead
     Management & Sales Automation CRM | Improve lead conversion and sales performance.
     Retrieved from: http://www.leads360.com/about-us/whitepapers/whitepaper-optimizing-
     call-attempts.aspx

7.   Noel-Levitz. (n.d.). 2010 Admissions Funnel Report. Noel-Levitz. Retrieved from: https://
     www.noellevitz.com/documents/shared/Papers_and_Research/2010/2010AdmissionsFunn
     elReport.pdf

8.   Getsatisfaction.com. (n.d.). Press Release. Getsatisfaction.com. Retrieved from: https://
     getsatisfaction.com/corp/company/press-releases/read/investing-in-facebook-twitter-
     pinterest-isnt-paying-off-for-brands

9.   Burstein, D. (2012). Landing Page Optimization. Marketing Experiments Blog. Retrieved
     from: www.marketingexperiments.com/blog/research-topics/landing-page-optimization-
     research-topics/ conversion-rate-improvement-helps-marketing-roi.html

10. Burstein, D. (2012). Landing Page Optimization. Marketing Experiments Blog. Retrieved
     from: www.marketingexperiments.com/blog/research-topics/landing-page-optimization-
     research-topics/ conversion-rate-improvement-helps-marketing-roi.html

11. Marketing Experiments Staff. (2012). Facebook Engagement Rates Continue to Surge in
     Q2. MarketingCharts: charts & data for marketers in online, Excel and PowerPoint formats.
     Retrieved from: http://www.marketingcharts.com/direct/facebook-engagement-rates-
     continue-to-surge-in-q2-22762/

12. Social Media Raises the Stakes for Customer Service . (2012, May 2). American Express.
     Retrieved from: http://about.americanexpress.com/news/pr/2012/gcsb.aspx

13. Email Open, Click Rates Seen Lowest During Work Hours. (2012). MarketingCharts:
     charts & data for marketers in online, Excel and PowerPoint formats. Retrieved from:
     http://www.marketingcharts.com/direct/email-open-click-rates-seen-lowest-during-work-

hours-22731/

14.   Getsatisfaction.com. Retrieved from: info.getsatisfaction.com/rs/getsatisfaction/images/ IncyteGroup_Whitepaper_Q32012.pdf

15.   Mobile Devices - New Media Trend Watch USA. (2013). New Media Trend Watch - Provided by the European Travel Commission. Retrieved from: http://www.newmediatrendwatch.com/markets-by-country/17-usa/855-mobile-devices

16.   Fathers Win Hearts of Commercial Viewers in Q2 2011. (2011). Newswire. Retrieved from: http://blog.nielsen.com/nielsenwire/media_entertainment/fathers-win-hearts-of-commercial-viewers-in-q2/

17.   Brenner, J. (2012). Pew Interent. Pew Internet: Social Networking (full detail). Retrieved from: http://pewinternet.org/Commentary/2012/March/Pew-Internet-Social-Networking-full-detail.aspx

18.   Skelton, A. (2012). Mashable. Social Demographics: Who's Using Today's Biggest Networks [INFOGRAPHIC] Retrieved from: http://mashable.com/2012/03/09/social-media-demographics/

19.   Kruger, J. (2010). Newsline. eMarketer reports catalogs are important to online retail. Retrieved from: http://pmanewsline.com/2010/03/12/emarketer-reports-print%E2%80%99s-place-in-multichannel-retailing-emarketer/#.UUcR3Vt4aRY

20.   eMarketer. (2010). Spurring Social Users to Search. Retrieved from: http://www.emarketer.com/Article/Spurring-Social-Users-Search/1007555

21.   Nielsen Blog. (2011). Winning Online is About Serving Your Audience, Not Impressions. Retrieved from: http://blog.nielsen.com/nielsenwire/online_mobile/winning-online-is-about-serving-your-audience-notimpressions/

22.   Zimbalist, M. (2010). Ad Age. Measure the Web Like TV and Brand Advertising Will Follow. Retrieved from: http://adage.com/digital/article?article_id=142173

23.   comScore. (2012). comScore Reports November 2012 U.S. Mobile Subscriber Market Share. Retrieved from: http://www.comscore.com/Insights/Press_Releases/2013/1/comScore_Reports_November_2012_U.S._Mobile_Subscriber_Market_Share

24.   Deloitte. (2009). Deloitte "State of The Media Democracy" Survey: Recession Intensifies America's Love for TV. Retrieved from: http://www.deloitte.com/view/en_us/us/dce196d6a8295210VgnVCM100000ba42f00aRCRD.htm

25.   InsightExpress. (2011). InsightExpress Mobile Advertising Effectiveness Norms 2007-2011 . Retrieved from: https://www.insightexpress.com/pdfs/InsightExpressMobile%20Norms_EOY%202011_final.pdf

26.   Leggatt, H. (2010). BizReport. Mobile Internet awareness lacking in Europe. Retrieved from: http://www.bizreport.com/2010/03/mobile_internet_awareness_lacking_in_europe.html

27.   Murphy, D. (2010). MobileMarketing. Mobile + Online Raises Brand Awareness, says IAB. Retrieved from: http://www.mobilemarketingmagazine.co.uk/content/mobile-online-raises-brand-awareness-says-iab

28.   Cahill, A. (2010). ClickZ. Catching up to Mobile. Retrieved from: http://www.clickz.com/3636125

29. Dejardins, M. (2009). SlideShare. Landing Page Optimization Study. Retrieved from: http://www.slideshare.net/MatthieuDejardins/landing-page-optimization-study-improve-conversions-on-lead-generation-campaigns-2484586

30. Wroblewski, L. (2010). LukeW ideation + design. "Mad Libs" Style Form Increased Conversion by 25-40%. Retrieved from: http://www.lukew.com/ff/entry.asp?1007

31. Dyer, P. (2009). Pamorama. Measuring Social Media ROI. Retrieved from: http://www.pamorama.net/2009/12/21/measuring-social-media-roi/#axzz2NFtwwUZ8

32. Del Ray, J. (2012). Ad Age. Advertisers Say What We're All Thinking: Social-Media Spending Is Going to Explode. Retrieved from: http://adage.com/article/digital/advertisers-thinking-social-media-spending-explode/233128/

33. Rodriguez, D. (2010). Bloomberg Buisnessweek. Why Design Matters. Retrieved from: http://www.businessweek.com/stories/2010-02-01/why-design-mattersbusinessweek-business-news-stock-market-and-financial-advice

34. Institute of Design at Stanford. (2013). Retrieved from: http://dschool.stanford.edu/

35. Gladwell, M. (2005). Gladwell.com. What is Blink about? Retrieved from: http://www.gladwell.com/blink/index.html

36. BBC News. (2006). First impressions count for web. Retrieved from: http://news.bbc.co.uk/2/hi/technology/4616700.stm

37. Chopra, P. (2010). Visual Website Optimizer. Signups increased by 60% after actually removing the signup form. Retrieved from: http://visualwebsiteoptimizer.com/split-testing-blog/signup-conversion-rate-ab-testing/

38. Chen, J. (2009). Usibility.gov. The Impact of Aesthetics on Attitudes Towards Websites. Retrieved from: http://www.usability.gov/articles/062009news.html

39. Marketing Experiments. (2013). Methodology. Retrieved from: http://www.marketingexperiments.com/methodology-marketingexperiments.html

40. Goward, C. (2009). Wider Funnel. The LIFT Model: Use These Six Factors to Increase Your Conversion Rate. Retrieved from: http://www.widerfunnel.com/conversion-rate-optimization/the-six-landing-page-conversion-rate-factors

41. Nielsen, J. (2010, March 22). Scrolling and attention. Retrieved from: http://www.useit.com/alertbox/scrolling-attention.html

42. Tennant, B. (2012). KISSmetrics. The Shocking Truth About How Web Graphics Affect Conversions. Retrieved from: http://blog.kissmetrics.com/shocking-truth-about-graphics/

43. BBC News. (2006). First impressions count for web. Retrieved from: http://news.bbc.co.uk/2/hi/technology/4616700.stm

44. Laja, P. (2012). Smashing Magazine. Quick Course On Effective Website Copywriting. Retrieved from: http://www.smashingmagazine.com/2012/05/18/quick-course-on-effective-website-copywriting/

45. Stanford Web Credibility Research. (2002). Stanford Guidelines for Web Credibility. Retrieved from: http://credibility.stanford.edu/guidelines/index.html

46. Towers, A. (2010). Usability Friction. Aesthetic Usability Effect. Retrieved from: http://usabilityfriction.com/2010/03/30/aesthetic-usability-effect

47.   Clarke, A. (2012). Usability Geek. 12 Typography Guidelines for Good Website Usability. Retreived from:http://usabilitygeek.com/12-typography-guidelines-for-good-website-usability/

48.   Harrod, M. (2008). Interaction Design Foundation. Chunking. Retrieved from: http://www.interaction-design.org/encyclopedia/chunking.html

49.   Porter, J. (2010). 52 Weeks of UX. Visual Hierarchy. Retrieved from: http://52weeksofux.com/post/443828775/visual-hierarchy

50.   Porter, J. (2010). 52 Weeks of UX. Visual Hierarchy. Retrieved from: http://52weeksofux.com/post/443828775/visual-hierarchy

51.   Soegaard, M. (2010). Interaction Design Foundation. Affordances. Retrieved from: http://www.interaction-design.org/encyclopedia/affordances.html

52.   Zapata, A. (2006). AttentionScan. Web Design is Settling Down. Thank God!. Retrieved from: http://www.idfive.com/blog/2006/09/web-design-is-settling-down-thank-god/

53.   Trenchard-seys, P. (2010). Short Bored Surfer. 11 Principles of Interaction Design explained. Retrieved from: http://shortboredsurfer.com/2010/08/11-principles-of-interaction-design-explained/

54.   Trenchard-seys, P. (2010). Short Bored Surfer. 11 Principles of Interaction Design explained. Retrieved from: http://shortboredsurfer.com/2010/08/11-principles-of-interaction-design-explained/

55.   IDSA. (2011). The Impact of Design on Stock Market Performance. Retrieved from: http://www.idsa.org/impact-design-stock-market-performance

56.   Norman, D. (2002). Jnd.org. Emotion & Design: Attractive things work better. Retrieved from: http://www.jnd.org/dn.mss/emotion_design_attractive_things_work_better.html

57.   Carleton University. (2011). HOT Labs. Retrieved from: http://www5.carleton.ca/hot/

58.   BBC News. (2006). First impressions count for web. Retrieved from: http://news.bbc.co.uk/2/hi/technology/4616700.stm

59.   Pick, Tom. (2007). The WebMarketCentral Blog. Retrieved from: http://webmarketcentral.blogspot.com/2007/08/roi-of-website-redesigns-per-forrester.html

60.   Marcotte, E. (2013). Ethan Marcotte. Retrieved from: http://ethanmarcotte.com/.

61.   Wikipedia. (2013). Jeffery Zeldman. Retrieved from: http://en.wikipedia.org/wiki/Jeffrey_Zeldman

62.   Garrett, J. J. (2006). JJG.net. About Me. Retrieved from: http://www.jjg.net/about/

63.   Wikipedia. (2013). Ajax (programming). Retrieved from: http://en.wikipedia.org/wiki/Ajax_(programming)

64.   Nielsen, J. (2012). Nielsen Norman Group. Repurposing vs. Optimized Design. Retrieved from: http://www.nngroup.com/articles/repurposing-vs-optimized-design/

65.   Wikipedia. (2013). Pareto Principle. Retrieved from: http://en.wikipedia.org/wiki/Pareto_principle

66.   Yahoo Finance. (2012). Number of Smartphones Around the World Top 1 Billion -- Projected to Double by 2015. Retrieved from: http://finance.yahoo.com/news/number-

smartphones-around-world-top-122000896.html

67.   Business 2 Community. (2012). Mobile Web Searches to Surpass Desktop Web Search by 2013. Is Your Website Ready? Retrieved by http://www.business2community.com/online-marketing/mobile-web-searches-to-surpass-desktop-web-search-by-2013-is-your-website-ready-0270678

68.   Frost, B. (2012). Net Magazine. Five responsive web design pitfalls to avoid. Retrieved from: http://www.netmagazine.com/features/five-responsive-web-design-pitfalls-avoid

69.   idfive. (2012). Idfive Wins Best In Class Award from: Interactive Media Awards. Retrieved from: http://idfive.com/about/news/idfive-wins-best-class-award-interactive-media-awards

70.   Angry Birds. (2012). Retrieved from: http://chrome.angrybirds.com/

71.   Crook, J. (2012). TechCrunch. Apple App Store Hits 650,000 Apps: 250,000 Designed For iPad, $5.5B Paid Out To Devs. Retrieved from: http://techcrunch.com/2012/07/24/apple-app-store-hits-650000-apps-250000-designed-for-ipad-5-5b-paid-out-to-devs/

72.   Erin, A. (2013). Site Pro News. Google Opens Up About Manual WebSpam Removals. Retrieved from: http://www.sitepronews.com/2012/01/03/the-explosion-of-the-mobile-web-is-your-website-ready-a-spnexclusive-article/

73.   Marketing Charts. (2011). Mobile Social Networking Shows Strong Growth in '11. Retrieved from: http://www.marketingcharts.com/wp/direct/mobile-social-networking-shows-strong-growth-in-%E2%80%9811-17362/

74.   Marketing Charts. (2011). 8 in 10 Smartphone Users Have Browsed Products. Retrieved from: http://www.marketingcharts.com/direct/8-in-10-smartphone-users-have-browsed-products-17665/?utm_campaign=rssfeed&utm_source=mc&utm_medium=textlink

75.   iPass. (2013). The iPass Global Mobile Workforce Report. Retrieved from: http://www.ipass.com/resource-center/surveys-reports/

76.   Marketing Charts. (2011). Tablets Go with TV. Retrieved from: http://www.marketingcharts.com/wp/television/tablets-go-with-tv-17672/

77.   Cellan-Jones, R. (2012). BBC Technology. Facebook 'likes' and adverts' value doubted. Retrieved from: http://www.bbc.co.uk/news/technology-18813237

78.   Cellan-Jones, R. (2012). BBC Technology. Facebook Q&A: The network justifies the cost of its "like" adverts. Retrieved from: http://www.bbc.co.uk/news/technology-18816674

79.   Oreskovic, A. (2012). Reuters. Facebook comments, ads don't sway most users: poll. Retrieved from: http://www.reuters.com/article/2012/06/05/net-us-facebook-survey-idUSBRE85400C20120605

80.   CNBC. (2012). AP-CNBC Facebook IPO Poll — Complete Results & Analysis. Retrieved from: http://www.cnbc.com/id/47391504/m

81.   CNBC. (2012). AP-CNBC Facebook IPO Poll — Complete Results & Analysis. Retrieved from: http://www.cnbc.com/id/47391504/m/page/6

82.   Edwards, J. (2012). Business Insider. DATA: Google Totally Blows Away Facebook On Ad Performance. Retrieved from:http://articles.businessinsider.com/2012-05-15/news/31704866_1_mark-zuckerberg-image-ads-advertising-platform

83.   Monetate. (2012). Ecommerce Quarterly (EQ). Retrieved from: http://pages.monetate.com/

eq/?src=M-W-Web

84. Kuchinskas, S. (2012). ClickZ. Social Media Ad Spending to Reach $9.8 Billion. Retrieved from: http://www.clickz.com/clickz/news/2174656/social-media-spending-reach-usd98-billion

85. Econsultancy. (2011). State of Social Report 2011. Retrieved from: http://econsultancy.com/us/reports/state-of-social

86. Wikipedia. (2013). Buzzword Bingo. Retrieved from: http://en.wikipedia.org/wiki/Buzzword_bingo

87. MDG Advertising Blog. (2012). Social vs Search [Infographic]. Retrieved from: http://www.mdgadvertising.com/blog/social-vs-search-infographic/

88. Taxi. (2013). The First Internet Banner Ever. Retrieved from: http://designtaxi.com/news/355819/The-First-Internet-Banner-Ad-Ever/

89. iab. (1997). IAB LANDMARK STUDY DEMONSTRATES WEB AD BANNER EFFECTIVENESS. Retrieved from: http://www.iab.net/about_the_iab/recent_press_releases/press_release_archive/press_release/4287

90. Dodd, M. (2010). MRWeb. Rebooting the Online Ad Metric - A new way to measure effectiveness. Retrieved from: http://www.mrweb.com/mrt/web10apr.htm

91. Leggatt, H. (2010). BizReport. Microsoft urges advertisers to adopt Dwell metric. Retrieved from: http://www.bizreport.com/2010/05/microsoft_urges_advertisers_to_adopt_dwell_metric.html#

92. Marketing Charts. (2010). Social Engagement Aids Branding. Retrieved from: http://www.marketingcharts.com/direct/social-engagement-aids-branding-12637/

93. Butcher, D. (2010). Mobile Marketer. Mobile ad campaigns 5 times more effective than online: InsightExpress study. Retrieved from: http://www.mobilemarketer.com/cms/news/research/5308.html

94. http://www.dmnews.com/use-a-brandresponse-marketing-model/article/86188/

95. Minthorn, T. (2004). Direct Marketing News. Use a Brand/Response Marketing Model. Retrieved from: http://www.dmnews.com/use-a-brandresponse-marketing-model/article/86188/#

96. Lipsman, A. & Radwanick, S. (2012). comScore. 2012 U.S. Digital Future in Focus. Retrieved from: http://www.comscore.com/Insights/Presentations_and_Whitepapers/2012/2012_US_Digital_Future_in_Focus

97. Nielsen. (2012). HOW AMERICANS ARE SPENDING THEIR MEDIA TIME... AND MONEY. Retrieved from: http://www.nielsen.com/us/en/newswire/2012/report-how-americans-are-spending-their-media-time-and-money.html

98. Bergman, C. (2012). Lost Remote. TV 'cord cutters' and 'cord nevers' increase, finds Nielsen study. Retrieved from: http://lostremote.com/cord-cutters-and-cord-nevers-increase-finds-tv-study_b25866

99. Stelter, B. & Chozick, A. (2011). New York Times. Paying a 'Sports Tax,' Even if You Don't Watch. Retrieved from: http://www.nytimes.com/2011/12/16/business/media/for-pay-tv-clients-a-steady-diet-of-sports.html?pagewanted=all&_r=0

100. Kilar, J. (2011). Hulu Blog. Q2. Retrieved from: http://blog.hulu.com/2011/07/06/q2/

101. Quantcast. (2013). Netflix.com. Retrieved from: http://www.quantcast.com/netflix.com

102. Mangano, J. (2012). comScore. Millennials' Digital Behavior. Retrieved from: http://www.comscore.com/Press_Events/Presentations_Whitepapers/2012/Millennials_Digital_Behavior

103. Peter Levine. (2008). an opening for the news media. Retrieved from: http://www.peterlevine.ws/mt/archives/2008/02/an-opening-for.html

104. Music Industry Facts and Figures (wiki). (2011). Changes in total album sales. Retrieved from: http://emuisemo.pbworks.com/w/page/34545425/Changes%20in%20total%20album%20sales

105. Rainie, L. & Duggan, M. (2012). Pew Internet. E-book Reading Jumps; Print Book Reading Declines. Retrieved from: http://libraries.pewinternet.org/2012/12/27/e-book-reading-jumps-print-book-reading-declines/

106. Kiser, P. (2010). Paul Kiser Blog. mag-sales.gif. Retrieved from: http://paulkiser.files.wordpress.com/2010/05/mag-sales.gif

107. Nielsen. (2011). CUE THE MUSIC DRIVEN BY DIGITAL, MUSIC SALES UP IN 2011. Retrieved from: http://blog.nielsen.com/nielsenwire/consumer/cue-the-music-driven-by-digital-music-sales-up-in-2011/

108. Bergman, C. (2012). Lost Remote. Grammys rock the ratings, set social TV record. Retrieved from: http://lostremote.com/grammys-rock-the-ratings-set-social-tv-record_b25926

109. comScore. (2011). Digital Omnivores: How Tablets, Smartphones and Connected Devices are Changing U.S. Digital Media Consumption Habits. Retrieved from: http://www.comscore.com/Insights/Presentations_and_Whitepapers/2011/Digital_Omnivores

110. Shields, M. (2011). AdWeek. Report: Facebook Ad Performance Is Abysmal. Retrieved from: http://www.adweek.com/news/advertising-branding/report-facebook-ad-performance-abysmal-126285

111. Lillie, K. (2012). TBG Digital. Global Facebook Advertising Report. RRetrieved from: http://clearslide.com/view/mail?iID=2TGN93ZFELA7QZ74ZHU9

112. O'Neill, N. (2010). AllFacebook. Facebook's Ad Revenue To Surpass $1.2 Billion This Year. Retrieved from: http://allfacebook.com/facebooks-ad-revenue-to-surpass-12-billion-this-year_b17168

113. McIntyre, D. A., Allen, A. C., Sauter M. A., Weigley, S & Uible, L. (2012). NBC News. Buy it now! America's biggest advertisers. Retrieved from: http://www.nbcnews.com/business/buy-it-now-americas-biggest-advertisers-887754

114. Kunz, B. (2012). Bloomberg Businessweek. Why GM and Other Fail With Facebook Ads. Retrieved from: http://www.businessweek.com/articles/2012-05-22/why-gm-and-others-fail-with-facebook-ads

115. The Wall Street Journal. (2012). GM Says Facebook Ads Don't Pay Off. Retrieved from: http://online.wsj.com/article/SB10001424052702304192704577406394017764460.html

116. Facebook. (2012). General Motors. Retrieved from: https://www.facebook.com/

generalmotors

117. Fleishman Hillard. (2012). Agency News: 2012 Digital Influence Index Shows Internet as Leading Influence in Consumer Purchasing Choices. Retrieved from: http://fleishmanhillard.com/2012/01/31/2012-digital-influence-index-shows-internet-as-leading-influence-in-consumer-purchasing-choices/

118. Faber, G. (2012). The End of Television. TV Everywhere. Will 2012 be the year of the multiscreen experience?. Retrieved from: http://www.theendoftelevision.com/tv-everywhere-is-taking-over-tv-will-2012-be-the-year-of-the-multi-screen-experience/

119. Grabham, D. (2011). Techradar. Apple iTV release date, news and rumours. Retrieved from: http://www.techradar.com/news/television/apple-itv-release-date-news-and-rumours-1045768

120. Frankel, D. (2012). PaidContent.Org. Nielsen: 1.5M U.S. households cut the cord in 2011. Retrieved from: http://paidcontent.org/2012/05/04/nielsen-1-5m-u-s-households-cut-the-cord-in-2011/

121. comScore. (2012). comScore Releases April 2012 U.S. Online Video Rankings. Retrieved from: http://www.comscore.com/Press_Events/Press_Releases/2012/5/comScore_Releases_April_2012_U.S._Online_Video_Rankings

122. comScore. (2011). It's a Social World: Social Networking Leads as Top Online Activity Globally, Accounting for 1 in Every 5 Online Minutes. Retrieved from: http://www.comscore.com/Insights/Press_Releases/2011/12/Social_Networking_Leads_as_Top_Online_Activity_Globally

123. Briel, R. (2012). Broadband TV News. Research: US viewers embrace PVRs. Retrieved from: http://www.broadbandtvnews.com/2012/03/02/research-us-viewers-embrace-pvrs/

124. Jacoby, A. (2012). Online Media Daily. Online Brand Ad Performance Isn't Subjective: You Deliver Or You Don't. Retrieved from: http://www.mediapost.com/publications/article/168516/online-brand-ad-performance-isnt-subjective-you.html

125. Gossage, H. L. & Goodby, J. (2006). The Book of Gossage (2nd edition). Copy Workshop.

126. Oran, O. (2011). The Street. 10 Top 'Branded' iPhone Apps. Retrieved from: http://www.thestreet.com/story/11185871/1/10-top-branded-iphone-apps.html

127. commpro. (2012). VIRAL VISIONARIES: 10 Top Branded Viral Videos. Retrieved from: http://www.commpro.biz/the-pulse/viral-visionaries-10-top-branded-viral-videos/#.UT89d9E4Uoo

128. Nielsen. (2013). Exploring the Consumer Media Univers. Retrieved from: http://www.nielsen.com/us/en/newswire/2013/exploring-the-consumer-media-universe.html

129. Selburn, J. (2011). Shipments of Internet-Enabled Consumer Devices to Exceed PCs in 2013. Retrieved from: http://www.isuppli.com/home-and-consumer-electronics/news/pages/shipments-of-internet-enabled-consumer-devices-to-exceed-pcs-in-2013.aspx

130. Mr. Magazine. (2011). Numbers are UP for new magazine launches in Third Quarter 2011. Retrieved from:http://mrmagazine.wordpress.com/2011/09/26/numbers-are-up-for-new-magazine-launches-in-third-quarter-2011/

131. IBM. (2011). What is Big Data?. Retrieved from: http://www-01.ibm.com/software/data/bigdata/

132. Lendenmann, K. (2012). Bridging the Digital Divide: How Marketers, Agencies and Publishers Can Evolve From Channel Specialists to Consumer Specialists. Retrieved from: http://www.iab.net/media/file/PulsePoint_Digital_Divide_Whitepaper.pdf

133. Indvik, L. (2012). Mashable. Online Ad Spending to Surpass Print for First Time in 2012 [Study]. Retrieved from: http://mashable.com/2012/01/19/online-advertising-surpasses-print-2012/

134. Stratmann, J. (2011). Fresh Networks. If 82% of TV ads generate negative ROI, why are we obsessed with social media ROI?. Retrieved from: http://www.freshnetworks.com/blog/2011/09/if-82-of-tv-ads-generate-negative-roi-why-are-we-obsessed-with-social-media-roi/

135. Carton, S. (2012). ClickZ. Anything You Can Do, the Internet Can Do Better. Retrieved from: http://www.clickz.com/clickz/column/2170021/-internet

136. Karlin, A. (2012). The Cross-Channel Conversation. 3 Traditional marketing Channels Digital Has Eclipsed. Retrieved from: http://blog.neolane.com/best-practices/3-traditional-marketing-channels-digital-eclipsed/

137. Manyika, J., Chui, M., Brown, B., Bughin, J., Dobbs, R., Roxburgh, C., & Hung Byers, A. (2011). McKinsey Global Institute. Big data: The next frontier for innovation, competition, and productivity. Retrieved from: http://www.mckinsey.com/insights/mgi/research/technology_and_innovation/big_data_the_next_frontier_for_innovation

138. IBM. (2011). What is Big Data?. Retrieved from: http://www-01.ibm.com/software/data/bigdata/

139. Hewitt, B. (2011). Forbes. Big Data: Big Costs, Big Risks And Big Opportunity. Retrieved from: http://www.forbes.com/sites/ciocentral/2011/05/27/big-data-big-costs-big-risks-and-big-opportunity/

140. Manyika, J., Chui, M., Brown, B., Bughin, J., Dobbs, R., Roxburgh, C., & Hung Byers, A. (2011). McKinsey Global Institute. Big data: The next frontier for innovation, competition, and productivity. Retrieved from: http://www.mckinsey.com/insights/mgi/research/technology_and_innovation/big_data_the_next_frontier_for_innovation

141. Wikipedia. (2013). HTTP cookie. Retrieved from: http://en.wikipedia.org/wiki/HTTP_cookie#History

142. Kolakowski, N. (2012). eWeek. Google Facing Investigation Over Safari Privacy Issue: Report. Retrieved from: http://www.eweek.com/c/a/Search-Engines/Google-Facing-Investigation-Over-Safari-Privacy-Issue-Report-446025/

143. Wikipedia. (2013). Filter Bubble. Retrieved from: http://en.wikipedia.org/wiki/Filter_bubble

144. Research Now. (2012) . Study Finds Marketers Struggle with the Big Data and Digital Tools of Today. Retrieved from: http://www.researchnow.com/en-US/PressAndEvents/News/2012/march/study-finds-marketers-struggle-with-the-big-data-and-digital-tools-of-today.aspx

145. Miller, D. (2011). Enterprises in Denial: Dealing with the Personal Data Deluge (Global Survey Results). Retrieved from: http://www.empirix.com/www/resources/media/pdf/whitepapers/WP_Opus_PersonalDataDeluge.pdf

146. IBM. (2011). IBM STUDY: Digital Era Transforming CMO's Agenda, Revealing Gap In Readiness. Retrieved from: http://www-03.ibm.com/press/us/en/pressrelease/35633.wss

147. Valentino-DeVries, J. (2011). The Wall Street Journal. Feds Can Get Twitter Users' Data Without Warrant, Judge Says. Retrieved from: http://blogs.wsj.com/digits/2011/11/10/feds-can-get-twitter-users-data-without-warrant-judge-says/

148. McAllister, B. (2012). The Atlantic. Addicted to Data: How an Obsession With Measuring Can Hurt Businesses. Retrieved from: http://www.theatlantic.com/business/archive/2012/02/addicted-to-data-how-an-obsession-with-measuringcan-hurt-businesses/253800/

149. Berret, D. (2011). The Chronicle. Battle Shapes Up as Dickinson State U. President Refuses to Resign. Retrieved from: http://chronicle.com/article/Battle-Shapes-Up-as-Dickinson/128551/

150. Keller, J. (2011). The Chronicle. Colleges Fight Google Ads That Reroute Prospective Students. Retrieved from: http://chronicle.com/article/article-content/128414/

151. Field, K. (2010). The Chronicle. For-Profits Spend Heavily to Fend Off New Rule. Retrieved from: http://chronicle.com/article/For-Profit-Colleges-Wage/124303

152. Wiseman, R. (2011). The Chronicle. Enrollments Plunge at Many For-Profit Colleges. Retrieved from: http://chronicle.com/article/Enrollments-Plunge-at-Many/128711/

153. LeadResponseManagement.Org (2009). THE LEAD RESPONSE MANAGEMENT STUDY OVERVIEW. Retrieved from: http://www.leadresponsemanagement.org/lrm_study

154. Cappex.com (2011). 6 Trends in Digital and Mobile Communications for College Admissions in 2011. Retrieved from: http://www.cappex.com/media/6digitalMobileTrends.pdf

155. Noel-Levitz. (2011) 2010 E-Expectations Report. Retrieved from https://www.noellevitz.com/papers-research-higher-education/2010/2010-e-expectations-report

156. Duck, S. (1997). Handbook of personal relationships: theory, research, and interventions. West Sussex, UK: John Wiley & Sons.

157. U.S. Department of Education National Center for Edcuational Statistics. (2012). Enrollment in Postsecondary Institutions, Fall 2010; Financial Statistics, Fiscal Year 2010; and Graduation Rates, Selected Cohorts, 2002-07 (NCES 2012-280). Washington, DC: Knapp, L. G., Kelly-Reid, J. E., & Ginder, S. A. Retrieved from: http://nces.ed.gov/pubs2012/2012280.pdf

158. Noel-Levitz. (2011) 2010 E-Expectations Report. Retrieved from https://www.noellevitz.com/papers-research-higher-education/2010/2010-e-expectations-report

159. Lehrer, J. (2012). The New Yorker. Goupthink: The brainstorming myth. Retrieved from: http://www.newyorker.com/reporting/2012/01/30/120130fa_fact_lehrer?currentPage=all

160. How Much Information?. (2009). How Much Information? 2009 Report on American Consumers (PDF). Retrieved from: http://hmi.ucsd.edu/howmuchinfo_research_report_consum.php

161. Wikipedia. (2013). University of Phoenix. Retrieved from: http://en.wikipedia.org/wiki/University_of_Phoenix

162. Wikipedia. (2013). List of United States university campuses by enrollment. Retrieved from: http://en.wikipedia.org/wiki/List_of_United_States_university_campuses_by_enrollment

163. Wikipedia. (2013). List of the largest universities by enrollment. Retrieved from: http://en.wikipedia.org/wiki/World%27s_largest_universities

164. Collis, D. (2002). New Business Models for Higher Education. Retrieved from: http://net.educause.edu/ir/library/pdf/ffp0101s.pdf

165. Wikipedia. (2013). Educational attainment in the United States. Retrieved from: http://en.wikipedia.org/wiki/Educational_attainment_in_the_United_States

166. Siegler, M.G. (2010). Tech Crunch. Eric Schmidt: Every 2 Days We Create As Much Information As We Did Up To 2003. Retrieved from: http://techcrunch.com/2010/08/04/schmidt-data/

167. Wikipedia. (2013). Credential inflation. Retrieved from: http://en.wikipedia.org/wiki/Credential_inflation

168. Khan Academy (http://www.khanacademy.org/)

169. University of the People (http://www.uopeople.org/)

170. Apple. Com (2013). iTunes U. Retrieved from: http://www.apple.com/education/itunes-u/

171. Sophia Learning (http://www.sophia.org/)

172. Hamilton, W. (2011). Los Angeles Times. For-Profit colleges face federal crackdown. Retrieved from: http://articles.latimes.com/2011/feb/06/business/la-fi-for-profit-colleges-20110206

173. MIT Open Courseware (http://ocw.mit.edu/index.htm)

174. Education Portal. (2013). Universities with the Best Free online Courses. Retrieved from: http://education-portal.com/articles/Universities_with_the_Best_Free_Online_Courses.html

175. Wikipedia. (2013). E-learning. Retrieved from: https://en.wikipedia.org/wiki/Online_education

176. The Sloan Consortium. (2012). Going the Distance: Online Education in the United States, 2011. Retrieved from: http://sloanconsortium.org/publications/survey/going_distance_2011

177. Wikipedia. (2013). Massive open online course. Retrieved from: http://en.wikipedia.org/wiki/Massive_open_online_course

178. edX (https://www.edx.org/)

179. coursera (http://www.coursera.org/)

180. noodle (http://www.noodle.org/)

181. Porter, C. (2013). The Wall Street Journal. College Degree, No Class Time Required. Retrieved from: http://online.wsj.com/article/SB10001424127887323301104578255992379228564.html?mod=e2tw

182. Wikipedia. (2013). Information wants to be free. Retrieved from: http://en.wikipedia.org/wiki/Information_wants_to_be_free

183. Google Trends (2013). Web Search Interest: curation. Worldwide, 2004-present. Retrieved

from: http://www.google.com/trends?q=curation

184. Rosenbaum, S. (2010). Mashable. Why Content Curation Is Here to Stay. Retrieved from: http://mashable.com/2010/05/03/content-curation-creation/

185. Schaffhauser, D. (2011). Campus Technology. Pearson Debuts Free LMS with Google Apps Integration. Retrieved from: http://campustechnology.com/articles/2011/10/13/pearson-debuts-free-lms-with-google-apps-integration.aspx

186. Blackboard (http://www.blackboard.com/)

187. Open Class (http://www.openclass.com)

188. moodle (http://www.openclass.com)

189. Sakai (http://sakaiproject.org/)

190. odijoo (http://www.odijoo.com/)

191. My I Course (http://www.myicourse.com/)